# THE ART OF
# ETHICAL THINKING

John H. Riker
The Colorado College

**University Press
of America**™

Library of Congress Catalog Card Number: 78-66415

To

Kaaren, Derek, Ethan

TABLE OF CONTENTS

PREFACE

This book is intended for people who are willing to question the way they are living, who seriously ask "How ought I to live?" and who do not know how to answer this question. This description fits a great many persons, for the problem of discovering how to live the best life possible is a fundamental one and the thinking needed to deal with it adequately is extremely difficult. Indeed, unless one becomes proficient in the use of concepts and methods of reasoning and cultivates certain dispositions and rational abilities, it is doubtful that he will be able to engage successfully in the art of ethical thinking--thinking whose purpose is to answer the question "How ought I to live?" The primary aim of this book is to elucidate the concepts, methods, dispositions, and abilities needed in ethical reasoning in hopes that it will help some people make better ethical decisions.

There are, of course, numerous books which have approximately the same goal. What distinguishes this treatise from others like it is, first, the development of a concept of morals which both allows for freedom in the choice of principles without being relativistic and demands substantial reasoning procedures without dogmatically assuming certain values. Second, it is an attempt to overcome the limitations of specific ethical viewpoints by the synthesis of major themes from the pragmatic, existential, and analytic traditions into a coherent theory. Third, and most importantly, it demonstrates that ethical reasoning must be grounded in certain character traits and abilities and specifies exactly what these traits and abilities are.

In this theme it is a marked departure from the concept of ethical thinking that has been dominant since the Enlightenment. In general, Western ethicists have maintained that anyone, regardless of his character traits and thinking abilities, could make correct moral decisions because everyone had access to some faculty--pure practical reason, general will, general sentiments, intuition, conscience, etc.--which would tell him what was right or wrong. Even though this notion of a special faculty is now almost universally denied, its effects are still so powerful that while contemporary ethicists ask "What constitutes ethical reasoning?" they do not explore what kinds of abilities and dispositions are needed in order to reason in the ways they propose. The ethical theory propounded here is a return to the ancient Greek notion that a person cannot determine what is good unless he develops certain habits of thinking and acting. Ethical reasoning does not occur in a vacuum or a disembodied soul, it occurs in people whose thoughts and acts are determined by the kinds of dispositions and skills they have developed. Hence, while the teleological biology of Plato and Aristotle is rejected and the traits seen by them as virtuous are quite different from those posited here, their belief that what is good can be discovered only by those people who have developed the requisite habits of thinking and acting is demonstrated to be true.

The elucidation of the methods of thinking required by ethics and the abilities and dispositions needed to perform these adequately will be set in the context of that problem upon which all modern theories of ethics have foundered and which only this kind of ethical theory can solve: the conflict of prudence and morals. If it is true that what is in one's self-interest is sometimes different from what morally ought to be done, then the question arises as to whether one ought to act morally or to promote his own interests. If one decides that self-interest is the highest criterion for action, then he is faced with the problem that there is no rational way to adjudicate conflicts of interest; these can be solved only by force. However, if it is maintained that everyone ought to be moral, then the question "Why be moral?" cannot be answered because one cannot say that it is in one's best interests to be moral, and it would be begging the question to say that it is morally good to be moral. Thus, a dilemma arises: either we have no rational means to solve conflicts of interest or we have no rational grounds for saying why someone should submit to moral adjudication.

This book will attempt to solve the problem of the conflict of prudence and morals in the following way. First, the prudential point of view will be examined to determine how an agent must think in order to discover what is in his best interest (Chs. 2, 3) and what skills and dispositions are required by this kind of thinking (Ch. 4). Next, the methods of reasoning required by the moral stance will be delineated (Chs. 5, 6) along with the personal traits and abilities needed to perform them (Ch. 7). Then, I will attempt to prove that the moral traits and abilities are a necessary development of the prudential ones (Ch. 8). That is, I will try to show that if the prudential person fully develops the traits and abilities needed by him to find what is in his best interest, then he must become a moral person. While this theory admits that what is in one's self-interest can in certain cases conflict with what is morally obligatory, it does not admit that the kind of person best able to determine what is in his interests is different from the moral person. Thus, it is the major goal of this work to determine what it means to be an ethical person and show why "living morally" is the only answer to the question "How ought I to live?"

I wish to acknowledge the help which my family, teachers, and friends have given me over the years in formulating the ideas of this book. Special thanks should go to Jane Cauvel, the late Glenn Gray, Lew Worner, and Connie Sharp for their invaluable criticism of my work and to my wife, Kaaren, Frank Krutzke, and Donna Werner for their help in the preparation of the manuscript. Most of all I must be thankful for Colorado College, whose humane and profound understanding of liberal arts education has provided a stimulating and supporting environment for my personal and intellectual growth.

# CHAPTER 1

## INTRODUCTION: THE PROBLEMS OF ETHICS

1.1  The fundamental question of ethics is also the most important practical problem for human beings: "How ought I to live?" It was poignantly raised by Socrates in the fifth century B.C. and ever since has served as a stimulus for many people to commence serious thinking about themselves and their actions. Why would a person raise this question? If the asking is not to be merely rhetorical or abstract, then there must be some problems, tensions, or anxieities that cause him to examine critically the way he is living. Many people raise the ethical question because they have suffered significant frustrations of desires and goals and thereby realize that something is wrong with the kinds of lives they are leading. Also, the question if often asked by people who are living reasonably satisfying lives but who wonder whether their lives are the best ones possible for them. They are moved to question the way they are living by a vision of what their lives ideally could be. However, many people who are constantly frustrated or who dream incessantly of ideal existences never raise the fundamental question of ethics. They do not ask the question because they believe that they are doomed to live as they do, that they cannot change the way they are living. So, while there are many kinds of situations which might cause one to question the way he is living, they will all involve a person's having three essential and interrelated beliefs:  that he has some control over his life and can, to some extent, plan it; that it is possible for him to choose various ways to live; and that the choices he makes make a difference--he can choose a better or a worse life.

The classical philosophers Plato and Aristotle thought that the most important fact about man, the one which distinguished him from all other creatures, was that he was rational and thus capable of directing his actions rather than having them controlled by the blind forces of his desires and environment. This is not to say that fate or fortune could be eliminated; for, than as now, fate plays an important and sometimes decisive role in a person's life. However, it was believed that if a person could rationally organize and understand his activities and desires, then he could lessen the power and dominance of fate. This belief that a person can control to some extent his life presupposes the belief that there are different ways in which an agent can live and that he is free to choose from among them. This does not mean that a person is completely free to choose any kind of life, for this is not true; but within a limited range of possibilities it appears that anyone has a choice of ways to act and react in the environment in which he finds himself.[1]  But believing that one is free to choose various kinds of lives will not lead a person to a critical examination of his existence unless he also has the further beliefs that of the ways of living open to him some are better than others and he can discover which these are.  If choice is to be significant, then it cannot be the same as chance or whimsey; it must involve decision, and decision is possible only if there are reasons for selecting one mode of action rather than another.

In other words, it appears that human beings can lead lives that are either the best possible for them or fail in various degrees to achieve this end and that if these ideal lives are to be attained, then people must attempt to control and plan their lives and their actions.  However, these attempts to direct a life and find what is good will be successful only if they are based upon adequate reasoning.  Unless one knows how to think well in making practical decisions, there is little reason to believe that he will discover those actions which will lead to his living the best life possible for him.  Thus, the fundamental question of ethics--"How ought I to live?"--demands that we be able to answer another question:  "How can I determine what is the best way to live?"

1.2  It will be helpful to give a more concrete account of what kinds of situations might cause one to ask "How ought I to live?"  A person's life can be described as a series of activities or events--arising in the morning, eating breakfast, reading the paper, talking with one's spouse about the news, dressing, going to work, doing a job, taking a coffee break, and so on.  These activities will be termed 'contexts' when they have purposes and are grounded by a set of rules.  The purposes may be trivial or ill-formed and the rules vague or not consciously formulated; however so long as there is some uniformity of behavior of the people engaged in an activity, it is a context.  Contexts can be particular or limited activities, such as those listed above, or they may be more general, such as being a father, being a librarian, being a British citizen, etc.  While these are not specific activities or events, they do have purposes and rules which govern the behavior of the people in them and necessitate that

---

[1]That man does have such a choice is a point challenged by some philosophers.  The question of freedom and determinism is a metaphysically intriguing one, but beyond the scope of this book.  All I need to assume here is that choices and decisions do make important differences in the way a person lives.

certain more particular activities be accomplished. Since contexts are so numerous and have such differing scopes, they can flow into one another, be arranged in a hierarchy of sub-classes and classes, and mutually support or conflict with one another. Contexts have a quasi-independent kind of existence, for although there would be no contexts without human beings, it is also true that there would be no human beings without contexts. If each of us had to rediscover and reinvent all the activities of our societies, we would not long survive. Generations of men come and go, but human activities with their purposes and rules endure.

We are not persons outside of contexts who then decide on what activities to enter; rather we always find ourselves inherently immersed in the various and multifarious contexts of our immediate lives and that our personal histories essentially consist of the kinds of activities in which we have participated. This means that one does not give himself his goals and rules for actions, but for the most part accepts and follows the rules and purposes of the context in which he finds himself. Insofar as the purposes of a context state what ought to be achieved and the rules distinguish the correct and incorrect ways of achieving that end, it can be seen that the context governs what values the person within it must hold vis-à-vis that activity.

The fact that people in modern societies are engaged in many and variegated contexts explains the paradox of why so many people have values which are unorganized, poorly formulated, barely conscious, and yet which seem to work quite well with little agonizing over them. While very few people are prepared to answer a question like "What is a good life?", there is no trouble in saying who is a good cook, or bridge-player, or actor, or toothbrusher, etc., because these values are given and engrained in the various contexts of which they are a part. Insofar as people's lives are basically lived in contexts with given contextual values that operate quite well within those activities, there seems to be no need to want to ask "How ought I to live?" or "Upon what principles should I base my life?"

Although being totally immersed in contextual existence seems to be an adequate way of living for many people, for others significant problems arise. What should I do when two contexts conflict, such as when I want to spend more time on philosophy and also desire to do many more things with my family? How should I decide which contexts to enter and which to avoid? How should I arrange and order contexts so that they issue into the best life possible for me? Are there any principles which should be followed in all contexts? These questions seem to call not for just another context, but for some kind of overriding discipline that can guide a person's actions and decisions as to what contexts to enter, how to organize them as to importance, how to solve

3

conflicts between them, etc. To state this in a more classical
way: many people seek a unity and rationale for their lives.
They often find themselves engaged in activities which have little
relationship to one another, and they have no idea whether their
involvement in them is the best thing they could be doing. The
vision occurs to them that they could arrange and plan their activities in some kind of meaningful and coherent pattern, that they
could be in control of their lives rather than being controlled
by the contexts in which they are submerged.

1.3 What then is needed? What kind of discipline or language is able to critique contexts and guide a person's choice in
such a way as to make him capable of deciding which contexts to
enter, which to avoid, and how to arrange them? Several aspects
of this discipline should now be evident. First, it will consist
of a prescriptive language--a language whose function is to guide
action. Our problem is practical--what should I do?--and the kind
of language which is constructed to answer this kind of problem is
language that either implicitly or explicitly prescribes actions.[2]
A purely descriptive language, such as science purports to be,
cannot help us. Knowing what the world is like is one thing;
knowing how to act in it is quite another. This dichotomy is
revealed in the common caricature of the brilliant professor who
knows the most complex facts about the world but who has no
practical wisdom--he can't get along in the world.

This, however, does not help us very much because, as we
discovered, every context involves at least some prescriptive
language--its rules. The prescriptive language we are looking
for is not just any one, but the highest or most authoritative of
prescriptive languages. That it must have this property of being
most authoritative is evident from the functions it has of settl-
ing disputes between conflicting contexts and of evaluating any
context. Economics might prescribe that we attempt to achieve
the greatest profits, but we can still ask "Ought we do what
economics prescribes?" Our church might prescribe that sexual
intercourse outside of marriage is wrong, but we can still ask
"Ought we to do what the church says?" Even if we want to say
along with Kierkegaard that one's absolute relation to the
Absolute is the most authoritative language, this is only because
we have already used a higher prescriptive language which told us

---

[2]This is not to beg the question against contemporary des-
criptivism. I understand the dispute between the prescriptivists
and descriptivists not to be over whether moral language is prescriptive, but whether moral prescriptions logically entail, or
are entailed by, a certain description. At this point in the
discussion this is not an issue; it will be fully raised in 1.4.

that we ought to let our actions be guided by this relation.
What is the most authoritative language? Traditionally it has
been termed 'ethics.' Although in various circles this word has
come to have more specialized meanings, I will use it in its
original sense as given by Aristotle: that discipline which seeks
to determine the principles of what it means to live a good life.

As such, ethics should be distinguished from the two sub-
classes which comprise it: morals and prudence. By 'morals'
will provisionally be meant 'that discipline whose goal is to
determine how we ought to act when everyone's interests are taken
into account,' and by 'prudence'[3], 'that discipline which attempts
to determine what an individual ought to do in order to achieve
what is in his best interests.' Although this terminology is not
fully justifiable by reference to ordinary language, which sometimes uses 'ethics' and 'morals' interchangeably, there is, nonetheless, a strong usage which suggests the definitions I have
given. At any rate, nothing substantial will be made to stand
or fall on this nomenclature; all that needs to be seen at this
point is that the questions about how one ought to act in relation to others and how one ought to act in order to promote his
own interests are subsidiary to the major ethical question of how
one ought to act.

1.4  So, ethics is that language whose prescriptions overrule all other prescriptions and which is supposed to answer the
question "How ought I to live?" Well, how ought I? One might
now expect to have presented to him the answers which ethics has
found to this question, but, alas, none will be forthcoming, for
by its very nature ethics can give none. Ethics does not give
any definite answers as to how people should live because one of
its most important rules is that any way of life is open to question, and if this is so, then it cannot prescribe one way of life
as unquestionably best. Ethics must involve freedom of decision
as to what is right and wrong.

To say that ethics involves 'freedom' means that a person
is neither linguistically nor factually compelled to accept a
given answer to "How ought I to act?" That is, ethical principles
cannot be fully justified by reference to facts or definitions
of ethical terms. Referring to facts cannot justify ethical
maxims, for to say that something is the case is one thing; to
say that it ought to be the case, quite another. Just because

---

[3]No word really seems appropriate here and I use 'prudence'
only because it is too cumbersome to write repetitively: 'discipline which attempts to determine one's best interest,' I realize
that 'prudence' has a connotation of 'smug carefulness and caution,'
but I do not mean to include this as part of my usage of the word.

it is a fact that people do commit adultery does not mean that they ought to. Even if it were a fact that many people would suffer greatly if someone did act 'x', this does not mean that he ought not to do it, for one can hold without logical contradiction both that 'x' causes suffering and that it is right. (Think of the case in which someone holds that the highest good for all men is to attain tragic wisdom and that this can come about only through suffering.)

Likewise, we cannot justify ethical claims by saying that they are true by definition, for even if there were generally accepted definitions of what the key ethical terms--'good,' 'right,' and 'obligatory'--meant (and at present there are no such definitions), all it would do is tell us how a certain people uses language, not what is good or right or obligatory. We can still ask if what they call right really is right. Just because in a certain society 'right' means 'getting pleasure by enslaving all other men who do not have the same skin color' does not mean that this practice is right.[4] Also, if taking an ethical stance meant that one had to follow some kind of principle like "Always act to increase human happiness," we could still ask "Why ought we to do that?" or "If that is what it means to be ethical, then why ought I to be ethical?" Insofar as we can sensibly ask these questions, it implies that the principle was not intrinsically part of ethics. For if it were, these questions could not sensibly be raised, since by definition, no 'oughts' can take precedence over an ethical 'ought.' So as not to get entangled

_____

[4]This doctrine has been recently subject to a strong criticism whose proponents (such as Max Black, P. Foote, J. Searle, and G. J. Warnock) argue that all evaluative language takes place in contexts or institutions and that these contexts define right and wrong actions such that the agent is not free to disagree with the evaluations in that context without committing nonsense. While it is true that within contexts evaluations are often analytically tied to facts, it is not true that these contextual evaluations lead automatically to prescriptions, for to say so is to assume that the prescriptions of that context cannot be overriden by other prescriptions (such as moral ones) and this is clearly false. If I knew that defeating my opponent at chess would make him commit suicide, I might very well say that x is the only move to checkmate him, therefore I ought not to make move x. Likewise, if I knew that the sharpest, strongest knife was made by a company that did not follow equal-opportunity hiring policies, then I might say that I ought not to buy it. No limited contextual evaluation is ever anything more than a prima facie prescription, and we are thereby free to reject any of these limited prescriptions.

in semantics, let me state this thesis without relying on the meaning of the word 'ethics.' Even if the answer to "How ought I to live?" comes to be generally associated with a certain set of principles, then human beings would still need a more authoritative prescriptive language (no matter what it is called) to evaluate those ways of acting to see if they really are the best way to live.

But it might be objected to this last point that there is at least one conceivable set of principles which, if followed, would eliminate any need for a more authoritative prescriptive language. Insofar as a 'need' implies that man has some kind of lack or dissatisfaction, it might be the case that if a certain set of principles were followed we would never feel a need to question our way of living. We would never feel a need to ask "How ought I to live?" because we would always be entirely satisfied with the way we were living. Aside from the extreme difficulty in imagining what set of values could possibly endure and be unchallenged in this world of precarious changes and contingencies, it is even harder to conceive of what people would be like if they never questioned their ways of life or wondered about what ways of life were best. This is not to make the value judgment that the life of a dissatisfied Socrates is better than that of a satisfied pig; rather it is to say that the acts of questioning the way we are living, wondering what kind of life is the best for us, and attempting to determine for ourselves what to do appear so fundamental to human existence that conceptually we have a difficult time imagining what man would be like without these experiences. Indeed, such philosophers as Nietzsche, Sartre, and Kant have asserted that critiquing one's way of life and making one's own decisions as to how he is to live rather than just following the dogmas handed down by others is the defining experience of man. "The unexamined life," Socrates held, "is not worth living." The question "How ought I to live?" seems to be an essential part of human experience. In order for an agent to ask this question in a way that is not merely rhetorical he cannot uncritically accept the principles of the authorities of his environment, even if these are passed down with definitional force. To ask this question is itself to assert one's freedom to decide for himself how he is to direct his actions.

1.5 However, if this freedom is to be at all meaningful then it must have some limits, some rules. To say that there are no rules or procedures by which we can distinguish a good choice from a bad one is to make choosing a senseless and meaningless activity equivalent to whimsey or chance. If freedom of choice is to be an important concept, then there must be some reasons for choosing one way rather than another. However, this conclusion will remain platitudinous until we know

what form this reasoning takes. Many philosophers have thought
that the kind of reasoning needed in ethics was that of deducing
value judgments from some self-justifying first principles.
These first principles were the ground of rationality in ethics--
if we could know them then ethics as a rational discipline was
possible, and if we could not know them then ethics was not
possible.

The problem with this concept of ethical reasoning is that
it puts us in a terrible dilemma. On the one hand, if there are
self-justifying first principles (and none have been unquestionably found yet), then it would be disastrous because it would
eliminate freedom in ethics. If there were a maxim which can be
known to be self-evidently true, then we could not rationally
question its validity; we would not be free to ask seriously,
"On what principle should I base my actions?" Yet, if there are
no self-justifying principles, then it seems that the base of all
ethical reasoning is arbitrary and the whole structure collapses.
Thus, it appears that men must have either no freedom in ethics
or no reason.

It is this dilemma that has generated much of the ethical
philosophy from Plato to the present day.[5] Subjectivists and
relativists, impressed by the failure of attempts to justify
moral claims and valuing freedom and individual self-determinaton
highly, have declared that ethics is not rational. On the other
side, objectivists, fearful of chaos and meaninglessness, have
contended that if there is any freedom involved in ethics, it is
only freedom to follow the correct ethical principle. However,
the negation of either side of the antinomy of freedom and reason leaves ethics in an impossible position. If there are no
rational grounds on which ethical decisions can be based, then
the autonomy and freedom of the agent which subjectivists have
so highly valued become equivalent to whimsey or taste, and
ethical choice becomes meaningless in that there are no reasons
for choosing one principle rather than another. On the other
hand, if full justifications were available for ethical principles then we would know what was right and wrong the way we
know the earth is round or that two and two is equal to four;
there could be no criticism of moral principles; we would never
have to ponder over what kind of life is good; we would simply
ask the computer what we ought to do, and be told.

1.6 This problem indicates that a different model of what

---

[5]This dilemma is the subject of one of the most important
recent books in ethics, R. M. Hare's Freedom and Reason.

8

reasoning means in ethics must be developed. Rather than regarding ethical reasoning as deductions from self-evident first principles, one could say that being rational in ethics means that one has to follow certain methodological rules in deciding what prescriptions to accept. For example, one might say that a rational ethical judgment is one which is the product of an investigation that examined all the facts of the case, attempted to foresee all the consequences of the intended act, tried to imagine how everyone's interest would be affected, etc. Thus, what this concept of ethics as a public discipline would give its participants is not a definite prescription of what way of life is best, but ways by which they can most rationally discover for themselves what actions and types of lives are the best for them.[6] This is certainly not an uncommon concept of rationality. Indeed, aside from traditional axiomatic systems of mathematics, most other kinds of disciplines do define rationality and justification in terms of following certain methods and rules for arriving at conclusions where this procedure does not involve deductions from given axioms. Thus we have the experimental method in the natural sciences, a complex interrelation of such procedures as referring to manuscripts, eye-witness reports, archeological evidence, and human psychology in history, rules for extrapolating from samples in sociology, etc.

This approach attempts to solve the antinomy of freedom and reason by maintaining that a person is free to prescribe any principle so long as that claim is the product of rational inquiry. That is, no prescription, regardless of how dastardly it may seem, can be dismissed a priori, and, likewise, no principle, however widely it is favored, should be accepted unless it has been subjected to the rules and procedures of ethical reasoning. Thus, rather than regarding freedom and reason as opposed, this view maintains that they require each other. Because no principles are given as self-evident or obviously true, man must use his rational faculties to determine what maxims to follow. Freedom without reason is blind; reason without freedom is useless.

1.7 However, all of this will remain abstract and unenlightening until it is determined what are the rules and methods of rational inquiry in ethics. Yet, as soon as we commence this quest to find what the rules and methods of ethics are, we immediately encounter another momentous problem: it is impossible to determine the rules of ethics because there is no such

---

[6]This concept that ethics should not supply substantial moral principles, but rather methods of reasoning that each person can use to determine his own ethical claims, has found strong modern adherents in the American pragmatists, especially John Dewey, and in the English analytical philosopher R. M. Hare.

discipline as ethics. There is no one language to answer the
question "How ought I to live?" Instead, the two sub-classes of
ethics--prudence and morals--exhaust the field of highest authoritative prescriptions. There is no further kind of 'ought' which
is an ethical 'ought' and which governs both moral and prudential
prescriptions. There are rules of rational prudence and rules
for making moral decisions, but no further set of rules above and
beyond these. The two kinds of reasons that have the most force
in directing one's actions are that the action is in one's own
best interests or that it is the most moral thing to do (which at
this point will be provisionally identified with acting in consideration of what is in the best interests of everyone). There are
no higher reasons than these, and, hence, ethics as a discipline
distinct from morals or prudence simply does not exist.

However, if ethics does not exist and morals and prudence
are discrete disciplines, then how can one decide what to do in
those important instances in which what is moral and what is in
one's interests appear to conflict? That the demands of morals
can be different from those of prudence is known by anyone who
has endured that agonizing struggle of attempting to decide
whether to seek his own happiness or to do that which he thinks
to be morally obligatory. A repressive government is following
a course which an agent deems morally wrong; yet, if he objects,
he knows he will be tortured and killed. He thinks it his moral
obligation not to participate in the activity, but also knows
that it is not in his best interests to be tortured and killed.
What should he do? Should he be prudential or moral?

There are three principal ways of solving this problem:
(a) when self-interest and morals conflict, one ought always to
do what is in his self-interest; (b) when self-interests and
morals conflict, one ought always to do what is moral; or (c)
one can deny that morals and self-interest do conflict (or, as a
variation of this, assert that the conflict can be eliminated by
social engineering).

The great strength of position (a) is its realism: it both
admits that there are conflicts of one's interest and those of
others and affirms that the only good reason anyone ever has for
doing anything is that it will further his own best interests.
This theory that self-interest is the only good reason for acting
finds its ground in the culture of Homeric and Classical Greece
and has since been a dominant and pervasive doctrine in Western
culture, reflected in such different areas as the earthly or
heavenly rewards for being moral of Christianity and the secular
individualism of Nietzsche. Its clearest expression is perhaps
in Book II of Plato's Republic in which Glaucon and Adimantus
state that in order for Socrates to show that people ought to be
just, he must demonstrate that justice is intrinsically and

necessarily in the agent's self-interest. However, when this theory of what is to count as a good reason for acting is combined with the belief that what is in one's best interests might not be the same as what is in the best interests of all, then the consequences appear disastrous. If men's interests do conflict and there is no rational way to adjudicate between them, then human interactions can only be governed by force. Might rules; there is no right. There are no grounds upon which we can condemn another person's or nation's actions except by saying that they are not in my or our interest; and this, of course, can carry no weight with one's opponents. The image which represents the final consequences of such egoistic ethics is found in the Odyssey of Homer: the land of the Cyclops where each is a law unto himself and where each must live in his own cave, for there can be no community. Although this individualistic kind of ethic has had strong proponents--perhaps Nietzsche is its most eloquent and forceful speaker--the fear of a chaotic society ruled by force and arbitrary desires has made it an unacceptable position for most people.

Yet, the opposite doctrine that people ought to do what is moral when there is a conflict of self and others also seems to have an insuperable difficulty, for it cannot answer the question "Why be moral?" It can't propose as a reason for being moral that this is the morally right thing to do, for this would clearly be begging the question; nor can it contend that being moral is in one's own self-interest, because by the very description of the position, this is false. Since the moral and prudential 'oughts' are the only authoritative ones, there seems to be no way of answering "Why be moral?" Even those theories such as Kant's which hold the dubious premise that a man must be moral if he is to be free and achieve human dignity are persuasive only to the extent that the individual thinks it best for him to be free and have dignity. Finally, the doctrines which contend that one ought to do what is moral because morality is based on a supreme authority, such as God, also cannot answer why one ought to obey that authority without referring to prudential reasons. Would one be so willing to follow God's laws if he thought them detrimental to his own happiness and also thought that whether or not he followed them made no difference as to any kinds of rewards or punishments he might receive?

The overwhelming problems with these first two positions have led many philosophers to deny that there really is a conflict of prudence and morality. They advance that self-interest and the interests of others are either in harmony or can be put into harmony by social engineering. "Honesty is the best policy." This position, if true, would solve many problems in a quite felicitous way. But in order to be acceptable it must give strong reasons for denying that the apparent conflict of interests is real. Here philosophers have produced a myriad of answers, but all have had to assert either of two very questionable doctrines. One position is that although virtue and happiness stand in an antinomous relation on this earth, there is an afterlife, be it in a kind of heaven or in a form of reincarnation, in which absolute justice reigns and the morally good are rewarded with happiness while those who were not so good are punished in accordance with their failures of virtue. Insofar as this position needs justifications both for the existence of a supreme being to mete out rewards and punishments and for an immortal soul, it seems a rather unprovable foundation on which to base the harmony of prudence and morals, and I shall discuss it no further.

This leaves as the remaining possibility a position which maintains that if and only if a person does what is moral or what is in the best interests of society can he achieve what is in his best interests during his lifetime. This certainly seems a dubious position in the light of the many persons who have suffered or martyred themselves for the good of their countries and the good of mankind. It is very difficult to see how it could be in one's best interests to be dead. One might try to reply to this that if the men had saved their lives by abandoning their principles, then they would have been totally miserable the rest of their lives and it really was in their best interests to die. But would they have martyred themselves if they had not developed a moral character? Was it in their best interests to develop this kind of character?

Another rejoinder is the Hobbesian one that it is in the best interests of everyone to have a civil society and that this can only be achieved if everyone is willing to place himself under certain moral obligations such as not to break the civil law, not to murder, rob, injure needlessly, etc., for only if everyone affirms the validity of common principles is there any basis for community. This appears to be sound since it is doubtful that anyone can achieve happiness without the security and organization of functions that societies offer, and it is doubtful that societies could exist unless their citizens were willing to take the moral point of view. But this does not really help us, for it only answers the question "Why should people in general be moral?" and not "Why should I be moral?" It might always be advantageous to be a part of a moral society, but it might be still more advantageous to be part of a moral society and not follow its rules when they conflict with one's interests. What must be shown is not just that it is better to belong to a moral society but also that one should always abide by its rules. Could not a man be better off by only pretending to follow the moral dictates of his society when they conflict

with his interests?[7] To declare that a person can't consistently
and rationally hold that everyone else ought to obey the moral
laws but that he shouldn't when it suits him will only bring the
retort that if this is what it means to be rational in morals,
then he is not interested in using this kind of reasoning.

One other major attempt to deal with this problem is that
given by Bentham and more recently, B.F. Skinner. It admits that
there is now a conflict of interests, but that this could be overcome by proper social programming. Because a person's interests,
aside from some basic biological ones, are contingent and a matter
of environmental conditioning, social engineers could program people so that they would receive ultimate satisfaction from doing
moral acts. That this might happen is indeed a possibility, but
it does not answer the philosopher's questions, for it can still
be asked whether people ought to have those interests or different
interests; whether the kind of happiness they are having is the
highest kind they could have. The term 'a person's best interests'
is not just a simple empirical one because something can be in
one's best interest even though he has no want for it and even
despises it. A person can say both that he has no interest in
classical music and that it might be in his best interests if he
did. Just because people become conditioned to believe that doing
the moral thing is in their own best interests does not mean that
it really is.

1.8 It is these kinds of problems with all the positions
on prudence and morals that have made many recent philosophers
avoid this question of the proper relation between them. A common position nowadays is that prudence and morality are separate
languages or disciplines and should be dealt with separately.[8]
Rules can be given for what one must do to take the moral point
of view or the prudential, but no consideration is given to the
relationship between them. What a person decides to do with his
own private life is one thing--he can entertain all kinds of
possible ideals for himself, any one of which he can choose without having to justify it by reference to other people's interests.
On the other hand, there is a definite set of rules which include
the consideration of the interests of others that must be followed
if one is to be moral. The reasons why anyone should be moral are

---

[7]For an excellent discussion of this problem see Kai
Nielson's article "Why Should I Be Moral?" Methodos, XV (1963).
This has been reprinted in Pahel and Shiller's Readings in
Contemporary Ethical Theory, Prentice-Hall, pp. 454-483.

[8]See Hare's Freedom and Reason, pp. 151-155, and P. F.
Strawson, "Social Morality and the Individual Ideal," in
Philosophy, vol. 37.

not given, for it is not the job of the moral philosopher to persuade people to be moral but only to clarify for them what rules and concepts are involved in taking the moral stance.

This kind of 'two spheres' theory reflects the point made earlier that there is no intermediary language between morals and prudence. But can it work? Can one separate his private life and ideal from his public dealings with others? Is it not true that the habits of character which we develop in either our private or public roles always have consequences for the whole of our actions? We cannot turn habits and states of character on and off like hot and cold water. As Aristotle well knew, a man can not separate who he is from what actions he does.

Even if we could separate our private lives from our interactions with others (a distinction I find barely intelligible), this still leaves us immense problems: "What should we do when our private ideals conflict with our moral principles?" and "How ought I to relate my moral life with the rest of my life?" For human beings who are trying to integrate the various activities and contexts of their lives into some kind of order or unity, it is not very helpful to say that there are two major spheres of authoritative 'oughts' which have different rules and purposes and which are not related. When a person asks "How ought I to live?" he is considering his life as a whole and is asking for some principles by which he can guide all his actions and activities. To say that he can live either prudentially or morally or with some kind of combination of these two authoritative prescriptive languages does not aid him, because what is being asked for is which way ought to be chosen.

1.9 These problems manifest why this book is concerned with 'ethics' rather than just with 'morals' and 'prudence.' It is not because there is some overriding discourse of ethics, but because there is a fundamental problem of how men are to organize and evaluate all their activities in some kind of coherent way. The art of ethical thinking is not just knowing how to determine what is prudentially good and what one morally ought to do; it is also knowing how to interrelate them and when one should supersede the other.

The sceptic may now have had too much. He might admit that this is indeed a very noble question and pursuit, but that without some kind of discourse in terms of which to answer it, it is meaningless to ask. As we have already admitted that there exists no separate normative language of ethics above and beyond morals and prudence, how can one possibly answer questions as to their interrelationships and rank of precedence?

The answer offered in this treatise will be in the form of a reductio ad absurdum argument.[9] It will commence by maintaining that the following two propositions are true: (a) that what is in one's self-interest is not identical with what is in the best interests of others; and (b) that the only good reason for doing anything is that it is in one's best interests. The justification for (a) is an immense amount of prima facie evidence witnessing the conflict of self and others. Proposition (b) is accepted as true by the failure of any other model of 'good reason for acting' to challenge it. The conclusion entailed by these two premises is that people ought always be prudential rather than moral--that prudence is the most authoritative prescriptive language. It is upon this conclusion that the reductio will work, for what I hope to demonstrate is that the intellectual tools and habits that are necessary in order for a person to achieve what is prudentially in his best interest lead irrevocably to his taking the moral stance.

The key to the argument will be the demonstration of the claim that both prudence and morals involve such difficult reasoning procedures that a person must have certain abilities and character traits in order to perform these processes adequately. In short, I hope to show that both the prudential person and moral person need the abilities to discern facts, to imagine how people feel as recipients of acts, and to reason logically, and that both need the traits of being objective, sensitive, thorough, and impartial. However, even though the abilities and traits needed in morals and prudence have the same names and are in general similar, they differ significantly in the particular form they take in prudence and in morals. What I wish to demonstrate is that if one attempts to develop the prudential forms of these traits and abilities fully, then they will necessarily develop into the moral forms such that the prudential person must become a moral person. This is not to say that being moral is always the most prudential thing to do [for this would contradict (a)], but that in order to be able to determine what is in his best interests a person must develop certain rational skills and traits, and the use of these necessitates that one take the moral stance, even if in individual instances taking that moral stance is not in one's best interests. Thus, while I admit that what is moral can and does in individual cases conflict with what is prudential and that a man might by chance live the best life for himself without being moral, what I will not admit is that developing a character that is best capable of satisfying its interests

---

[9]A reductio ad absurdum argument is one which attempts to prove a proposition by assuming its opposite and showing how such an assumption leads to a contradiction.

is different from developing a character that is moral.

In this attempt to prove that morals is the highest prescriptive language we must not commit either the fallacy of giving morals a normative definition or the fallacy of making morals a point of view in which there is little place for reasoning, for we have already discovered that the most authoritative prescriptive discipline must both allow for freedom in the choice of values and demand that rational procedures govern the choosing.

Hence, our task is threefold. We must first explore the standpoint of prudence in order to see what methods of thinking one needs to determine what is in his best interests. With this information we can then attempt to discover what personal abilities and traits are necessary for carrying out those methods. Next, we must examine the moral point of view to discover what its reasoning procedures are and what kinds of traits and abilities are needed to perform them. And, finally, in order to answer our original question--"How ought I to live?"--we must understand why the moral traits and abilities necessarily develop from the prudential ones, and why the only way one ought to live is as a moral person.

PART I: PRUDENCE

CHAPTER 2

VALUES AND ENDS

2.1  Let us now assume that the only good reason for doing
anything is that it is in one's best interests.  But what does
'in one's best interests' mean?  An action will be said to be in
one's best interests if, more than any other act he can do at the
time, it aids him in achieving the most satisfying life possible
within the limitations of his circumstances.  Although what is
meant by 'satisfying life' must be purposely left vague (for to
give it a definite form or concrete descriptive meaning would be
to presuppose an unjustified value judgment), the following, at
least, can be said.  A person's life consists of the experiences
he has, and thus to speak of a 'satisfying life' is to refer to
an existence which minimally has some satisfactions.  A 'satisfaction' will be defined as the fulfillment of a desire or
desires with 'desire' being used here as a generic term for any
feeling which seeks some kind of completion, and, hence, includes
all wants, wishes, needs, likes, longings, etc.

It might be thought that in contrast to the very difficult
enterprise of determining what is objectively or morally right
and wrong, finding what is subjectively best is an easy matter:
all one needs to do is determine what his desires are and then
learn ways to satisfy them.  We may not know what is right, but
we do know what we like and what we want.  Yet, as anyone who has
seriously undertaken this task of determining what is in his best
interests knows, it is an exceedingly complicated task.  Desires
conflict such that the satisfaction of one means the frustration
of another.  Likes and dislikes change drastically over the course
of a lifetime.  Wants wax and wane in strength and intensity.  We
would be better off not having some desires that we do have,
while others that we do not have we would be better off having.
Indeed, it was not so much the problem of the conflicts of individuals within society as the widespread ineffectiveness of people to deal with their desires and to achieve their own good
that stimulated Socrates and Plato to initiate ethical philosophy.

The basic problem in determining what is in one's best
interests, then, is the discovery of which of one's desires ought
to be satisfied and to what extent.  This problem is solved by
the formulation of values, for values represent that class of

17

desired objects, events, or experiences which one thinks ought to be realized. They are the tools by which a person directs his actions in that they prescribe which desires ought to be fulfilled and which ought to be subverted. So, in order to determine what is in one's best interests, a person needs to find those values the actualization of which will bring him the maximum of satisfaction.

This is no easy task, for, as we should expect from the previous descriptions of contextual living and desires, a person's values are usually uncritically accepted and in a state of massive confusion. Myriads of limited contextual values are intermingled with some transcontextual values of varying scopes of application. There is very little order. Many values are so engrained that we are only semi-conscious that we are following them. Other values, while consciously realized, are so poorly formulated that in marginal cases we do not know whether they apply or not. Rather than being harmonized and mutually reinforcing, one's values often tend to be atomized and mutually destructive. Even more important is the fact that most of the values have not been chosen for their efficacy in aiding a person attain satisfaction; rather they have been uncritically accepted from the various communities of which he is a member. As such they may be aids or significant hindrances in helping a person live a satisfying life.

Is this picture too bleak? The only way one can tell is by performing a personal experiment in which he asks himself the following questions. What are the major values I hold which determine for me what contexts I enter, how to arrange these contexts, and how to solve conflicts between them? What reasons do I have for believing those values really are in my best interests? What is the relationship between these main values? Which ones take precedence in the case of conflict? Why? If the reader is at all like the author, then he will have excruciating difficulties in answering these questions.

2.2 How can one transform this multifarious conglomeration of uncriticized values into some kind of ordered whole, such that his values will be able to direct his activities into a pattern of the most satisfying life possible for him? Some philosophers have held that the only way this can be accomplished is by destroying or questioning all of one's values and commencing completely anew without any normative presuppositions. This, however, is impossible, for one can determine which values to follow only when he has some standard by which to evaluate those values, and this standard is itself a value judgment. If this standard is also to be questioned, then there will be no criterion by which to choose values, and thus choosing will become arbitrary and capricious; it will have no greater likelihood for discovering what is in a person's best interests than uncritically received opinions.

Rather than a total questioning of all our values, the procedure we ordinarily use when critically affirming or rejecting values is one in which we balance one value against another. If we find that value x contradicts y in a certain case and feel that y is more desirable than x, we reject x. Although this kind of procedure tends to be piecemeal and oriented to solving crises as they arise, it could be very helpful to the person trying to organize the important contexts of his life, if he could use it to discover which of his values took precedence over which others. With this knowledge he could then arrange his values in a hierarchical way and this would permit him to be cognizant of those values which he esteems the highest and which he can use as criteria for evaluating his other values. If this method is the appropriate one, then the major question becomes how to determine which of the values one holds should serve as the highest standard for the rejection or affirmation of his other values.

The first step in this determination is to distinguish between those things or experiences which are valued as a means to other things or experiences and those which are valued as ends in themselves. I value going to the dentist not because I intrinsically value having my teeth drilled, but as a means to prevent my experiencing far more pain in the future. However, I listen to music not because of any consequences that this experience might have, but because I value this experience in and of itself. These classes of ends and means need not be mutually exclusive as there can be experiences which are valuable both for themselves and for their consequences.

It should be obvious that it is ends which provide the criteria by which we choose and evaluate means. A 'good means' will be one which brings about the desired end with the fewest negative consequences for other desired ends. I wish to attend the concert tonight and can get there via several means: walking, taxi, or public transportation. As it is quite far, walking would make me too fatigued to listen well and would take up valuable time. The taxi, while the most enjoyable, would cost so much that I could not purchase other things that I want. Considering that the public transportation is almost as fast and far cheaper, I choose this as my means of getting to the concert. This is the common way most of us reason, and manifests that it is ends that are the most important values we have.

What is an 'end in itself'? We use the word 'end' in many

ways, but its meanings most likely to be confused are 'terminus' and 'that which is desired for itself.' Many contexts have ends in the sense of termini which are not ends desired for themselves. For instance, I might say in answer to an inquiry as to why I painted a friend's house that I did it to make money. I wanted this money to buy a chair, and I bought the chair so that I could relax in it. While getting money, buying the chair, and relaxing in the chair are all ends in the sense of termini, it is only the experience of relaxing in the chair which is the end desired in itself (assuming that I do not find getting money and buying things to be intrinsically enjoyable activities). It is only those experiences which are desired for themselves that can be valued as ends in themselves.

This last statement implicitly contains a judgment which is agreed upon by philosophers and which is of the utmost importance to grasp: only experiences can be ends in themselves. Although we often talk as if it were things which we desired for themselves --money, a house, children--it is clear that what we really want is the experiences we expect to have with those objects or people. It makes no sense to desire an object for oneself but not expect to experience it in any way. What we seek is not money but the having of money, or the spending of money, or the touching of money, etc. That it is only experiences which are valued for themselves and that things can be valued only as means for achieving them is a commonplace; but the failure to recognize the implications of this for one's ethical thinking is widespread and often costly. The problem is that we often do our value thinking in object-language (language which names objects, rules, contexts, etc. without specifying what experiences are associated with them) rather than experience-language (language which describes experiences). It is quite natural for us to do this, as object-language is often a shorthand for experience-language and is much easier to use. For example, a person can say that what he wants is to be a doctor, to own a home, to be married, and to have children without carefully thinking through what experiences are involved in each of these contexts. This is because 'being a doctor,' 'owning a home,' 'being married,' and 'having children' all carry with them strong positive emotive meanings, and are thus often assumed to be good without any attempt to explore the kinds of experiences involved in them, experiences which might prove quite unfulfilling for a person with certain desires, abilities, and dispositions. Thus the first rule in thinking about ends is to translate crucial object-language into terms of experiences. What kinds of experiences are involved in having children? getting married? entering a profession? Only when detailed and accurate answers to these questions have been given can one start to decide rationally to what kinds of activities he ought to commit himself.

2.3 The fundamental question, then, in determining what values one should choose as standards for the affirmation or rejection of other values is "What kinds of experiences do I value as ends in themselves?" But this formulation of the problem is not adequate in that 'kinds of experiences' is ambiguous. 'Kinds of experiences' might refer to certain determinate activities such as eating candy, seeing a painting, walking through the woods, etc. or more general types of experiences such as those involving happiness, pleasure, joy, or contentment. We usually think about what experiences we value in terms of the determinate activities. If a person is asked what kinds of experiences he esteems, almost never will he say "happy ones" or "pleasant ones," but rather "playing golf" or "reading novels." It is taken for granted that everyone values happiness or pleasure or contentment--what is wanted is what kinds of experience give a person happiness, pleasure, etc.

But this procedure will not work, for the kinds of determinate experiences we find valuable in themselves are too numerous and varied. If one defines his ends in terms of such limited activities, then he will be unable to give them a hierarchical structure and they will, hence, be of little use in guiding his decisions about what general contexts to enter, how to arrange them, or how to solve conflicts between them. In order to handle these kinds of problems, we need criteria to evaluate these more determinate activities and thus must refer to some more general types of ends.

Why not evaluate determinate activities simply in accordance with the amount of satisfaction they give? This suggestion has the opposite fault of being too indeterminate, for although I have used the word 'satisfaction' indiscriminately to cover happiness, pleasure, and joy, and these terms are often used interchangeably, they, nevertheless, have uses which indicate that there are several different types of experiences and arrangements of experiences that are possible as ends, and that it will make a difference to a person's life which kind of experiences he favors. To substantiate this claim and to clarify some of the key concepts in ethical reasoning, I will attempt to delineate what I take to be the three general kinds of experiences and types of lives they entail that men have found most worthy to be sought as ends in themselves: pleasure, happiness, and ecstatic joy.[1]

---

[1] Although there are other terms we use to express positive attitudes towards kinds of experience, I find in general that they are either very broad terms of commendation covering all these experiences, such as 'satisfaction' and 'felicity,' or else subclasses of one or more of the three I have mentioned, such as 'contentment,' 'delight,' and 'gratification.'

2.4 Pleasure: Of the three terms, 'pleasure' has the widest scope of application, for while happiness and joy will both involve feeling pleasure, feeling pleasure need not involve being happy or feeling joy. Because so many kinds of experiences can involve one's feeling pleasure, it is extremely difficult to define or describe. Some pleasures like the gratification of sex or hunger are definite feelings or sensations localized in the body which have corresponding pains as their opposite states. However, there are other pleasures associated with such activities as walking, listening to music, and talking with a friend which do not appear to be definite sensations, to be localized in a part of the body, or to have corresponding pains. Although there is this diversity of pleasures, it nonetheless seems true that pleasure is not experienced simply as a separate or isolated feeling, but always as connected with definite activities. Pleasures are 'pleasures of'--pleasures of eating, pleasures of thinking, pleasures of sensing, etc. Aristotle expressed this when he said that "Pleasure completes the activity not as the corresponding permanent state does, by its immanence, but as an end which supervenes as the bloom of youth does on those in the flower of their age. . . . Without activity pleasure does not arise, and every activity is completed by the attendant pleasure."[2] Thus it can be said that pleasure is like an aura that permeates activities which are desirable when pleasure completes them and a matter of indifference or avoidance when pleasure is absent (think of the activity of eating sweets when one is healthy and when one has teeth with open decay).

Of the activities which can give pleasure there seems to be no limit. Such different experiences as scratching an itch, hearing an owl's hoot, contemplating the mathematical formulas of quantum physics, even the experiencing of bodily pain (for the masochist) can be activities which give certain people pleasure. In order to experience some pleasures, one need do no more than have sensations; in order to experience others, great labors are needed to put oneself in the position necessary for having them, such as long philosophical training in order to experience those pleasures connected with understanding a philosophical issue in depth. With all these kinds of pleasureful activities possible, how is a person to tell which ones are better than others? Two kinds of answers have been traditionally offered: (a) pleasures differ in kind and some of these kinds (usually intellectual pleasures) are superior to the others; (b) pleasures differ only in quantity and those with more quantity are superior to those with less.

---

[2]*Nichomachean Ethics*, Book 10, Ch. 4.

22

Both of these theories are deficient. The attempt to discriminate pleasures into higher and lower kinds, besides being phenomenologically suspect, cannot work without maintaining that there are other characteristics which the higher experiences of pleasure have that make them more valuable. But this is to deny that it is pleasure and only pleasure which is intrinsically valuable, for it is pleasure and something else which makes the experiences worthwhile. Depending on what the something else is, we will probably arrive at a theory of happiness (pleasure which comes with the attainment of an ideal of excellence) or of joy (pleasure which comes from the union with the prime force of the universe). This objection has led most hedonistic philosophers to hold that activities can be evaluated only according to the amount of pleasure they give, this being determined mainly by the intensity of the pleasure and its length of duration. But just because one thinks that experiences of pleasure are good does not mean that he must also maintain that more intense and lengthy pleasures are always better than those that are shorter and of less intensity. There seem to be many times when we prefer a less intense or shorter pleasureful activity, not simply because of possible negative consequences a more intense or longer experience might have, but because our mood desires a gentler or quieter pleasure. Different activities and their concomitant pleasures are fitting or appropriate at different times of our daily lives, and often our choice of activities has little to do with either the length or the intensity of the pleasure we expect to have. This does not mean that a person who seeks pleasure as his end cannot hold that he ought always to seek the activities which provide him with the most intense and lengthy pleasures, but only that such a criterion does not follow simply from recognizing pleasure as the intrinsic end.

If one takes pleasure to be his highest value, then his task is to find what kind of life will give him the pleasures he most desires. As the experiencing of pleasure need not depend upon the fulfillment of any ideal of human excellence or any other definite way of life, the kinds of activities and lives open to the person seeking pleasure are innumerable. It can be a life with carefully planned goals or one of living for the day to day pleasures. It might mainly involve activities of sensual pleasures or be centered around the delights of intellectual inquiry. Hence, the person who seeks pleasure as his end will have a great deal of freedom to choose that way of life which is tailored to fit his desires, dispositions, and abilities. He need not worry about whether he is experiencing right or wrong kinds of pleasure; all that matters is that his activities continue to give him the kind of pleasures he desires.

2.5 Happiness: Although 'happiness' and 'pleasure' are often used interchangeably, there are several uses of 'happiness' and 'happy' which indicate that this concept is quite different from that of pleasure. For instance, we almost never substitute 'pleasant' or 'pleasing' for 'happy' in the expressions "Happy Birthday" and "Happy New Year." Why? My guess is that birthday and New Year celebrations were traditionally very important events of the renewal or rebirth of the person or year and that wishes were made not just for the person's experiencing or the year's bringing varied and atomistic pleasures, but, rather, that the person would have and the year would bring a form of continuous and lasting well-being. The difference of the queries "Are you happy?" and "Are you pleased?" manifests this same point. "Are you pleased?" is almost always used to ask about a particular reaction to a particular event, while "Are you happy?" often is used to enquire about a person's general state as it enters into all his activities.

Another linguistic datum indicating this difference between the concepts of pleasure and happiness is that, except for the strange case of the masochist, it is quite difficult to say both "I am in pain" and "I am feeling pleasure," while there is nothing odd about saying "Even though I am in pain, I am still very happy" (think of a woman giving birth). What these uses seem to indicate is that happiness is more a matter of a long-term and constant state of a person's character and is not so dependent upon his being engaged in certain determinate kinds of experiences. Whether one feels pleasure or not can fluctuate from activity to activity; happiness seems to be far more stable and capable of qualifying even the most painful of activities.

If one is inclined to think that etymologies of words contain some of the wisdom of the people of that language, then there is further evidence for this difference between happiness and pleasure. Both 'happiness' and 'happens' are derived from the same root 'hap' which means 'chance' or 'luck.'[3] What appears to be intended is the belief that the attainment of happiness is a matter of chance or luck, and this makes sense only if 'happiness' is interpreted as a continuous and lasting state of well-being. With the possibility of such uncontrollable events as disease, famine, accidents, wars, etc., occurring at any time, it indeed takes a great deal of luck to be prosperous for a lifetime. As the people of Thebes say at the end of Sophocles' play Oedipus Rex: "We must call no one happy who is of the mortal race, until he has crossed life's border, free from pain." Thus, while the experiencing of pleasure is tied to participation in definite activities and fluctuates with these, it seems that happiness must

---

[3]This etymological connection between luck and happiness is found in at least several other languages, for instance in the German 'Glücklichkeit' and 'Glück' and the Estonian 'õnn.'

24

be continuous over a long period of time.

But how is this to be understood? If happiness must be some kind of experience in order to be an end in itself and experiences are constantly changing, how can happiness be a kind of continuous experience? The answer to this question is contained in the other important difference between pleasure and happiness: that in order to attain happiness a person must strive to achieve an ideal of excellence.

Although to feel pleasure one usually need only satisfy some desire, this does not seem to be true for the experience of happiness, for assessing whether a person, oneself or another, is happy involves not only discovering that his desires are satisfied, but also that his desires are of the right kind. Not only is the happy life a satisfying one, it is also good. This is expressed in the definition of happiness given in the Shorter Oxford English Dictionary: "Happiness is the pleasurable content of mind which results from the success or attainment of what is considered good." For instance, if the only major desire a person had was to get pleasure from being high on heroin and he succeeded in satisfying this desire for his entire life, while never experiencing the joys of friendship or self-development or perception of physical beauty, many of us would say that he was not happy, or at least had not experienced the significant kinds of happiness that other humans had. Is it better to be a pig satisfied or a Socrates dissatisfied? According to the criteria of pleasure, it will depend on what one's desires are; according to the criteria for happiness, a pleased pig cannot be fully happy.

While semantically this aspect of the meaning of happiness is not present in all the uses of the term and its adjective, nonetheless it is important to see that the kind of experience here being portrayed as the ultimately valuable one (no matter what it is called) is the experience of knowing that one's acts and his character are fitting or appropriate according to his ideal of what a human life should be. What occurs in the experience of happiness is a complex relation between a held ideal and the actions and events of a person's life. When it is seen that the actual acts and events correspond to the ideal, then a feeling of fittingness and well-being pervades the experience as its dominant quality. Insofar as the ideal will probably involve future unattained goals, neither the correspondence nor the sense of well-being will be complete; but this does not mean that a strong degree of happiness will not be felt, for the person can realize that it would not be fitting for him to have fully attained the goals of his ideal at that time. Indeed, one of the attractive features of happiness is that it can grow as the ideal becomes better fulfilled and thus can give a sense of progress and development which is hard to achieve with the more atomized satisfactions of pleasure.

The reasons why the achievement of an ideal is an important aspect of happiness are several. One is that this is what gives a human being stability, continuity, and direction to help guarantee that he will continue to feel satisfaction over a long period of time (ignoring extreme ill-fortune) and not be so subject to the vicissitudes of definite experiences to give him pleasure. A person can experience happiness not only while he is engaged in the definite activities which fulfill the ideal, but also whenever he cares, consciously or semi-consciously, to reflect on his life. As this reflective experience (which is usually semi-conscious) can occur over and over again so long as one's actions have been in line with his ideal, one can continuously experience happiness, and this explains how happiness can be both a kind of experience and a state of well-being. Also, it is the feeling of fittingness that can allow a person to say in moments of suffering or tragedy that he is nonetheless happy, for he can still regard his actions as fulfilling his ideal.

If happiness is that experience which a person decides is ultimately valuable, then he must formulate a general ideal of excellence, determine which concrete activities or contexts will best achieve that ideal, and then choose the means by which to enter those contexts. This is quite unlike the concept of the life of pleasure which allows a carefree and unstructured way of living if this is what a person desires. Many people think that the two are equivalent--that they can experience the most pleasure by attempting to actualize an ideal of excellence, but this need not be so and often is not so, for adherence to an ideal can often commit one to a destiny of great suffering and/or premature death. If one seeks pleasure as his highest goal, then he is free to change expediently his ideals and positions as the forces of his environment change and thus preserve his opportunities for future pleasures. But the man who develops his character around the achievement of an ideal cannot so readily change without destroying the life he has built, and might, like Socrates and Thomas More, have to choose death rather than the abandonment of the ideal. The rewards of happiness may be great; but its dangers and sacrifices are also quite real. To devote oneself to an unworthy ideal or to try to actualize that ideal in ineffective ways can doom a person to a life of folly or frustration. It may be true that a good deal of luck is needed to attain a complete life of happiness, but it is also true that careful reasoning on these matters can do much to lessen the powers of fate and to put one's chances for happiness more into his own power.

2.6 Ecstatic Joy: While everyone has had some experience of pleasure and most have felt the kind of limited happiness that

26

accompanies the actualization of a project, the religious experience of ecstatic joy is a much rarer and less sought experience. 'Ecstatic joy' will be used to refer to that experience in which a person believes himself to be in some kind of mystical union with the universe or with the supreme power of that universe. What a person really does experience in ecstasy is a very difficult and important question, but one which cannot be argued here. What is important to this discussion is what people who have had this experience believe happens and what kinds of desires it satisfies in them.

Those who advance joy as the most valuable of human experiences often use the following mode of argument. Joy is the only completely satisfying experience because it is the only one in which the fundamental drive of all men can be fulfilled: the desire to survive. All men want to survive, want to persist in their being, and this drive is not limited to a definite period or number of years, but is unlimited--man wishes to exist indefinitely. However, all men know that they are finite and are going to die and thus in ordinary experiences this desire for indefinite existence cannot be fulfilled. Not only is this true for ourselves but it is also true of all the objects or persons we love, since we realize that they, too, are contingent and finite and will some day no longer be. But to love them is also to desire that they remain in existence. This anxiety always tempers our love and frustrates our ability to achieve full satisfaction in any experience. Thus, insofar as we seek only to attain happiness or pleasure by experiencing finite objects, persons, or events, this will in an essential way leave our most fundamental desires unsatisfied.

The only way in which these problems can be overcome, according to this view, is by the extraordinary and rationally indescribable experience in which the finite and infinite become one. It is only in this experience that the person can fully realize that he and all else are essentially part of the infinite and in which his drive for indefinite existence for himself and his loved ones is absolutely satisfied. Once this experience is had, then all other experiences can give far more pleasure and happiness because they are understood in relation to the infinite and can be enjoyed without any anxieties as to their contingencies.

If one thinks that this kind of experience is veridical and agrees that it is very important to have this kind of experience, then the question becomes how does one go about putting himself in a position to experience the infinite. Here there is much controversy. Some hold that there is nothing one can do to have the mystical experience; it happens by the grace of God and can happen to anyone at any time regardless of who he is and what he has done. If this is so, then it is obviously impossible to direct one's

activities around having this experience as their goal, for it is
a matter entirely outside of a person's choosing. However, there
are other schools of thought which hold that someone can greatly
improve his chances of having this experience if he correctly pre-
pares himself for it by following a certain pattern of life. Thus
we have the way of Buddha, Kierkegaard's movements of faith, the
life of self-denial of some Western mystics, Dionysian communal
rituals of wine and dance, etc. To choose to enter one of these
ways of life in hopes of having the religious experience is an
extremely serious decision of immense consequence, as it usually
will affect every activity in which a person participates. In
many instances the kind of life required will demand that one
eliminate or frustrate many of his other desires for worldly pleasures in order to devote himself entirely to the infinite.
Although many of these ways demand that some kind of commitment of
faith be initially made if there is going to be any chance of
experiencing ecstatic joy, it seems folly to sacrifice, on blind
faith alone, years of possible rich and fulfilling experiences in
hopes of having an experience that may never occur.

Before the commitment of faith is made, it would seem wise
for the prospective participant to do several things. First, one
must consider the claims for why this experience is thought to be
so important: does one have overriding fears and anxieties about
the contingencies of himself and the world? How important are
these in comparison to the rest of his desires? Second, one
should attempt to gain all the information he can on the mystical
experience and attempt to decide whether such an experience really
is an encounter with the primal force of the universe or only a
supreme case of wish-fulfillment. Finally, if after these analy-
ses the person finds that he wants to try to have this experience,
then he should carefully examine the various 'ways' available to
him and attempt to decide which will probably be the most successful.

The experience of ecstatic joy is quite different from either
pleasure or happiness. Unlike pleasure, it is not a completion of
some determinate activity which under different circumstances
might occur without pleasure's being felt, but rather is one self-
contained and fully integrated event. The mystical experience
and joy are so interrelated that one cannot occur without the
other. Unlike happiness, joy does not involve a complex comparison of an ideal life with the actual events of one's own life,
nor can joy be called forth as when we wish to feel happy and
thus reflect on our lives. Likewise, the life directed toward
the experience of joy can be very different from lives seeking
pleasure or happiness. Although a person might experience the
most pleasure in his life by seeking and having the mystical
experience, or might get the most happiness by having as his

ideal the religious person seeking union with God, neither of these need be so. The harder of the cases to see is that of happiness, for if a man decides that above all he wants to experience joy and also thinks that living in way x is the best way to do this, then it appears that x must also be considered by him to be an ideal of excellence. But the cases are different. With happiness one follows an ideal as an end in itself; the way of life needs no further justification than that it is ideal. But with joy the ideal is only a means to the end of having the mystic experience, and if one came to believe that there was a better way of bringing on the mystical experience than the way he is now living, he can change the pattern of his life without altering completely his ethical values. Also, a person might believe that way of life x was the ideal way to live (and this did not include having the experience of joy) but be so haunted by fears of death that he decides to seek the religious experience rather than follow x. That is, he could understand his fears as pathological and resign himself to living a life less than ideal in order to assuage those fears.

2.7 The point of these sketches of pleasure, happiness, and joy has been to show that 'seeking satisfaction' is not a definite enough end, for while pleasure, happiness, and joy all are kinds of satisfying experiences, they are nonetheless, all different and can demand different ways of life. Although people often desire to have all these experiences, there are many cases in which they conflict and in which the experiencing of one frustrates the others. Anyone, who has had the common experience of both wanting to relax in a dull and undemanding activity and feeling guilty and uneasy about doing so because it does not fit into his ideals, knows how the lives of pleasure and happiness can conflict. The indecision and tensions that often arise when a person oscillates between seeking pleasure and happiness indicate the need to decide which of these experiences to consider primary. So, although a person may hold all of these kinds of experiences to be ends in themselves, it is important that he develop some kind of priority among them so that he can solve conflicts and better direct his life.

How, then, is one to choose which of these kinds of experiences (or any other general kind of experience which a person finds exceptionally satisfying) to have as the criterion by which he can order all his other values? This problem presents a paradox, for in order to make the decision it seems one must have a criterion by which to distinguish which of these experiences is the most valuable. But by the very nature of the problem there can be no criterion, for what is being decided is precisely what shall be the highest standard of value. All reasoning must originate in some presuppositions, and in prudential reasoning about values it commences with what one accepts as the kind of experience he deems to be ultimately valuable.[4] A person can reason about what activities or contexts will best actualize this end, but he cannot deduce the ultimate end from any higher premises. As Aristotle says, "We deliberate not about ends but about means to ends."[5]

How, then, can a person decide which end is best? Is there one end which is self-evidently better than the others, as Aristotle thought happiness was, or Bentham, pleasure or Spinoza, joy? As far as I can see there is no one kind of experience which can be shown to be universally and necessarily best for all men. It certainly isn't true that any one of these is considered best by definition; otherwise my very raising of this question would appear linguistically nonsensical. Nor is it true that all men in fact desire or want one of these ends more than the others. Some people not only are unconcerned about unifying their activities around an ideal but would feel terribly restricted and limited by such a life; others desperately need to believe that only certain patterns of living are right and eschew pleasureful activities that do not fit into the structure of these ideals. Still others are constantly restless and disturbed until they are taking steps to know God in an ultimate way. It seems that different people have different basic desires and thus need different kinds of experiences to satisfy them.

Does this mean that one's most important choice--his decision of what kind of experience to seek--must be made arbitrarily and whimsically? It need not be, for when a person is in a position to make this decision he is not a tabula rasa or an empty receptacle; rather, he has experienced many kinds of satisfactions and will have developed certain more or less permanent dispositions and skills which, while subject to alterations, cannot be completely changed. With these experiences, dispositions, and skills as data, the first step in choosing one's primary end is to examine the kinds of satisfying experiences he has had in an attempt to determine which ones have been the most fulfilling. Self-examination of almost any kind is not an easy matter; minimally what is required in this case is an understanding of the concepts of happiness, pleasure, and joy, and an adeptness at analyzing one's experiences for underlying similarities. Are one's most satisfying experiences characterized by the achievement of a

---

[4]This is one of the insights of intuitionism: our highest prescriptions cannot be derived from any other premises. But this does not mean that we come to them through some kind of direct intuitive insight.

[5]*Nichomachean Ethics*, Book III, Ch. 3, 11.

goal, by multifarious kinds of pleasures, or by the feeling that one was becoming closer to the primal force of the universe? If one can answer this question, then he will know what general kind of experience has been most fulfilling to him in the past and can use this as a basis for predicting what will be the most fulfilling for him in the future.

Attempting to imagine what it would be like for one to live the various kinds of lives conceptually entailed by the different experiences one is considering as possible ends is the second step in choosing one's highest value. This is necessary to prevent being overwhelmed by contingent and temporary factors and misled by not fully recognizing the consequences of choosing a kind of experience as an end. As a youth one may be caught up in the pleasures of adventures and new experiences and detest having to abide by some ideal set for him by his elders, but when he attempts to imagine a whole life consisting of having one pleasure after another without any goal or structure to them, he might then find that he has an underlying need to structure his experiences around an ideal. On the other hand, a person who finds that experiences of accomplishing a goal have most satisfied him might yet decide to seek pleasure when he thinks about the sacrifices, limitations of experiences, and dangers of confrontation that will be involved in trying to live an ideal life. Perhaps, a person will find none of the experiences he has had can ground a life that would fully satisfy him, in which case he should, through literature or communications with others, attempt to discover some other esteemed experience and attempt to imagine what it would be like to have that experience and a life based on it.

But now a problem arises which will take our investigation into far murkier waters. In attempting to choose between happiness and other ends, it seems necessary to decide whether or not there is an ideal way for one to live. Although the impression may have been given that any ideal would do, this simply is not true. Minimally, a person must believe his ideal is the right one for him, because if he thought it to be arbitrary then it would have very little power to direct his life or serve as a principle for solving the conflicts of desires. But just believing the ideal to be right without having a justification for doing so can also be catastrophic in that the ideal could falter when severely challenged. For a person to have lived a substantial portion of his life according to an ideal and then find that he can no longer believe in it is an extremely painful experience that often involves viewing many of one's sacrifices and toils as having been in vain. Supporting this view, that one can choose inopportune ideals, are the many cases in which people fulfill their ideals but are not satisfied or happy. How many women who reach their ideal of marrying, living in a comfortable home, and raising wonderful children also remain profoundly frustrated? How often does one hear of men who achieve their ideal of becoming millionaires and who then commit suicide or become tremendously despondent? These examples manifest that before one can seriously opt for happiness, he must first determine if there really is an ideal way of life for him.

To maintain that a certain way of life is ideal involves, I believe, claiming two things: that the achievement of this way of life will cause the individual to experience the maximum satisfaction possible for him, and that this is the fitting and right way for a human being to live. The way philosophers have traditionally attempted to prove that one way of life is superior in both satisfaction and fittingness to others has been to maintain that all human beings have a single, basic, all-pervasive drive which more than anything else defines what it means to be human and the fulfillment of which is maximally satisfying. The ideal life is then defined as the one which has as its goal the total fulfillment of this drive. The history of philosophy abounds in illustrations of this kind of argument. For instance, Plato in his Symposium portrays the ideal life as the seeking of beauty in all its forms and directed towards the consummatory instance of this experience in the seeing of the essence or form of beauty. This way of life is ideal because it is only these experiences of beauty which fundamentally satisfy the most powerful and pervasive force in all men: Eros. Aristotle's ideal of the rationally directed life culminating in the contemplation of metaphysical truths is based on his theory that the strongest drive in any natural being is to seek the telos (end) of its species and that the telos of man is to be rational. The reason Spinoza posits the ideal life to be one of progressively gaining knowledge of the universe until one experiences the intellectual love of God is that this is the only means by which man can satisfy his ultimate drive to continue his existence indefinitely, and Nietzsche's ideal of the creative self-ruled individual is founded on his belief that the ultimate force in the world is the will-to-power, that is, an ultimate need to determine one's own actions and self.

Since at this point in the general argument we are only concerned with finding what is in one's own interests, the claim that a certain way of life is right or fitting will not be dealt with where this means more than its giving a maximum of satisfaction. Usually something more is meant in terming a way of life 'fitting' and this is that it is also morally right or justified. Because this kind of claim cannot be adequately discussed until the moral point of view has been delineated, what we now need to explore is the proposal that there is in every man a basic drive whose complete fulfillment is maximally satisfying and whose partial fulfillment is satisfying to the extent of the fulfillment and frustrating to the extent of non-fulfillment.

But one might have a preliminary objection that such an examination of basic human drives is quite unnecessary in that all one really needs in order to make this kind of argument prudentially sound is to find that he has a basic drive whose fulfillment would give him the maximum of satisfaction. Whether or not any other person has such a drive makes no difference. This objection is valid but raises the question as to whether one could possibly find so fundamental a drive by examining himself only, for several significant kinds of problems arise when one attempts to do so.

First, there is the problem that one can base his conclusion about what will always and most fully satisfy him only on what experiences he has already had, and these can be misleading in that one is often periodically dominated by desires which do not continue to be so pervasive later in his life, such as the sexual desire of youth or the quest for adventure of early adulthood. Second, if there is a drive pervasive in all experiences, then it must be extremely general and abstract (i.e., for self-realization, beauty, survival, self-determination); yet one is so involved in the particular and concrete aspects of his own experiences that it is very difficult to penetrate through these to get to the level of abstraction needed to find a basic drive. Finally, if one only engages in self-analysis, then he can have no independent test to see if his conclusions are correct. How is he to be sure that he has correctly identified and described his drive? How can he check his opinions against some kind of objective criteria? He can't.

These problems have greatly bothered philosophers who, on the whole, abhor having to base such an all-important thing as an ideal of life on such contingencies, and who have, therefore, sought to find a drive so fundamental to all human beings that man could not be conceived without it. Whether there is such a drive the fulfillment of which is maximally satisfying for every person is a question certainly worth examining, for if there is such a drive, then knowledge of it would be critical in determining what is in one's own interest. But this is where the analysis begins to get very complex, for we soon learn that we cannot properly examine human nature without also examining nature itself, as man cannot be understood apart from the world of which he is a member. Indeed, almost all the philosophers who put forth ideals of life also construct metaphysical systems of the universe to support and elucidate their views of human nature in which those ideals are based.

We have now plunged deeply into the murky realm of metaphysics, as we needed to if we were not going to limit arbitrarily the analysis of self. This would present no problems if one could with some certainty attain knowledge of the ultimate metaphysical entities and their relations. However, as the history of philosophy has made manifest, the more general and abstract one's categories of explanation become, the less they are amenable to experiential testing and the less certainty they have.

Thus it appears that we go beyond the uncertainties of self-analysis only to end up in the even larger uncertainties of metaphysics. What can possibly be gained by doing so? Several things, perhaps, can be achieved by a study of metaphysics in relation to ethics. First, even though a person may doubt that the concepts and categories of certain metaphysical philosophers have universal validity, he might find them very helpful in analyzing his own experiences. Second, I believe that we all have certain basic metaphysical concepts by which we view the world, that we are mainly unaware and uncritical of them, and that these categories exert a powerful influence on how we think and act. Explorations into metaphysics might help make one to become aware of what his own metaphysical presuppositions are and give him more options as to how to view the world.

But in the end, we must come back to the basic dilemma of generality and certainty. The more general and all-encompassing our search becomes, the less certain are our conclusions. But the price of certainty is limitation of perspective, a limitation which might cause us to miss our quarry and be ignorant of that aspect of ourselves which is most important. Whether to base a prudential ethic on a limited study of oneself that has some certainty, on a general concept of human nature which is much less certain, or somewhere in between is a problem that each individual must solve for himself and which will probably be decided, in the words of William James, by his "sentiment of rationality." However, if one refuses to leave the realm of concrete experiences, then it is doubtful he will ever find an ideal way to live, for such ideals as self-realization, rational development, or seeking beauty imply that one thinks he has some fundamental and comprehensive drive towards these ends, and this can only be discovered by exploring one's experiences at the most general and abstract level.

2.8 Once these steps of analyzing one's experiences, imagining what kinds of lives he could lead, and, perhaps, making an examination of human nature have been taken, then all a person can do is look at the data and say: "It is this experience and this kind of life that I find most satisfying and appealing, and therefore choose it as my end." This end is not logically deduced from the data for there will always be a logical gap between what we find is the case (a statement about what we do desire or find satisfying) and what we ought to do (a prescription about what is desirable or satisfactory). This is/ought gap manifests what

makes ethical thinking so excruciating: not even one's best reasoning about himself and his experiences can guarantee that he
will discover what really is the most satisfying life for him.
People and their environments have unknown aspects and can change
in unforeseeable ways. The possibility always exists that there
is a way of life that we can't imagine but which would give us
the most satisfaction if we had known about it and chosen it.

Thus the objection that this mode of argument is logically
fallacious is true--ends can't be deduced from factual premises--
but unhelpful, except in that it reminds us of our fallibility. A
person still needs to choose which experience to seek as his ultimate end, and he can do this either by fiat or by a thorough examination of his experiences and character and by imagining what
his life would be like, seeking the various ends open to him. To
act by fiat is to put one's chances for satisfaction totally into
the hands of fortune; to base one's actions on self-knowledge and
insightful imagination is to make as rational a decision as is
possible and to attain some control over one's life.

The choosing of an end is extremely important, for without
this our practical reasoning would be headless--undirected and
without a goal. But choosing an end is only the gateway to the
realm of practical wisdom and is often not the place where many
of the serious errors in finding one's own good occur. This is
because the choices of ends are few and many men have strong pre-
reflective dispositions toward the end that they would have chosen had they attempted a reflective inquiry. It is discovering
what concrete activities will best actualize the chosen end that
causes these further difficulties and it is to these problems
that we now must turn.

# CHAPTER 3

## VALUES AND MEANS

3.1 While having an end is necessary if one's prudential thinking is to have coherence and a central direction, this kind of reasoning will remain ineffective until one also knows what kinds of activities will actualize that end. Happiness, pleasure, and joy do not just occur by themselves (except, perhaps, when joy occurs by grace); they must be generated by a person's performing certain acts or being involved in certain contexts. Will playing ball or reading a book give one more pleasure today? Will becoming a parent help one attain his ideal of self-realization or will it hinder it? Is self-denial the best way to the experience of God? Unless one knows what definite activities will cause him to feel happiness, pleasure, or joy and what resources and acts are needed in order to produce these definite activities, he will be unable to evoke these ends. Hence, in order to be an effective prudential agent one must understand what means are necessary to effect the kind of experience he has chosen for his end.

The actions we perform as means to attain our ends may be of two kinds: activities which are in themselves unsatisfying or those which are intrinsically satisfying. That is, some labors done to achieve an end are indifferent or painful for their agents, while others not only lead to the desired ends but are also ends in themselves. All things being equal, it is obvious that the preferable means are those which both secure the conditions of future satisfactions and are enjoyable in themselves. Attempting to find activities which are both a means and an end in themselves cannot be stressed too highly in this age whose techniques of mass production have created an enormous number of unfulfilling jobs and which concomitantly has fostered as the paramount criterion for the evaluation of functions the amount one is paid for doing them. To earn one's living doing a detested task, whatever one is paid for it, is to condemn a large portion of a person's life to frustration; while finding a mode of work that both intrinsically fulfills one and gives him the basis for satisfying his material needs is to have a firm ground for continuously attaining one's end.[1]

---

[1] It is in the works of John Dewey that this theme of finding coincident means and ends is most strongly described and advocated. See especially his _Experience and Nature_.

The problem of eliciting what is in one's best interests now appears to be very complicated, for we have found that one needs to determine not only what activities will directly satisfy him, but also what means are required in order to engage in those contexts, and whether any of these means can themselves be ends. And when one considers that there are usually a great many activities that can satisfy a person, that each of these activities requires a number of means to bring it about, and that these activities and means will have supporting, indifferent, or destructive relationships with one another, then he might be at a loss to know how he can make a prudential decision at all. This complexity often drives people to make prudential decisions on a piecemeal basis, concentrating now on satisfying this desire and now on satisfying that desire. That such a policy can be disastrous is exemplified by the case of Joe who, at a certain point in his life, found himself strongly wanting to live in a stately, exquisitely furnished home, and who became a business executive in order to attain the money needed to buy such a house. Although he attained his goal of getting the home, he discovered that his somewhat satisfying job was so demanding that it eliminated or significantly reduced other activities that were very important to him, such as spending relaxed time at home with his family, becoming thoroughly immersed in literature and art, having rewarding personal encounters with his friends, etc. Because Joe isolated his desire for a stately home from other crucial experiences, he reached his goal of living in such a home, but lost his chance for achieving a maximum of satisfaction in his life. What is needed, then, is not a kind of piecemeal approach but an inclusive and comparative examination of all the activities that have given or might give one satisfaction, the means necessary to achieve them, and the interrelationships--supportive or destructive--of these activities and resources.

How is a person to perform this reflective examination? What procedures and methods should he follow to get the best possible answers? The place to begin the examination is, obviously, with the particular end one has chosen, for depending on which kind of experience a person is seeking, he will need to understand different kinds of methods and data. For example, the person pursuing pleasure need not know how to work with ideals, while this is the most crucial knowledge for the person wanting happiness. Thus, even though many of the methods will be similar no matter what end is being sought, the soundest procedure will be to treat the problems and methods connected with each end independently of the others.

3.2 The most important task for the person seeking pleasure is to determine what contextual activities will give him the maximum of the kinds of pleasures he desires over a projected lifetime. To discover what these are a person needs to examine his desires, dispositions, abilities, and, in particular, what has already given him pleasure. The only other possible basis for predicting what might give one pleasure would be to see what gives other people pleasure and surmise from this that the same experiences would give him pleasure, too. However, it is a fact that the same activity can evoke pleasure in some people, indifference in others, and pain in still others. In order to determine whether an activity which gives some other people pleasure will also please oneself, a person must discern if his needs, character, and abilities are similar to those of the people experiencing the pleasure, and this cannot be accomplished unless one has an understanding of himself.

Since desires are usually so indefinite that one often does not know what he wants until he has experienced satisfaction in some concrete activities, the best place to commence one's self-examination is with an inventory and understanding of the kinds of experiences which have given him pleasure. However, as soon as we attempt to take this inventory, a problem arises in that, while one can usually remember certain experiences as having been pleasing, he might not know how to describe them so as to manifest those properties of the experience which were significant in producing pleasure for him. For instance, one might remember the seeing of a certain red rose as especially satisfying; but should this experience be described as "the seeing of a red rose," "seeing roses," "seeing flowers," or, perhaps, "experiencing nature." Different descriptions of this experience could lead to quite different courses of action, such as going only to see gardens with red roses, going only to rose gardens, going to see flowers whereever one can, or exploring the many different facets and forms of nature. The properties involved in any experience are indefinitely numerous and none of them comes with a little tag saying "It is I which causes pleasure." How is one then to know which description best captures the properties of the experience which makes it valuable to him?

The main way to determine which properties are essential is by making hypotheses as to what characteristics or sets of characteristics one thinks were critical in causing him to feel pleasure in an experience and testing them against other of his experiences in which they occurred to see if they, too, were pleasant. For instance, the person in our example might find that walking through a flowerless forest was always an indifferent experience and thus know that the key property was not "experiencing nature." He might also remember that every time he saw flowers of any kind he was pleased, and this would tend to indicate that for the purposes of determining possible future pleasures, the experience with the rose would best be described as an instance of "seeing flowers." Determining the essential properties that make a kind of experience satisfying is very important, for misdescriptions

can be catastrophic. To describe a series of pleasureful experiences as "the courtship of a woman," when for future satisfactions
it was really best described as "the courtship of Jane," might
make one miss a lasting and fruitful relationship. On the other
hand, to describe the series as "the courtship of Jane," when it
was just the pleasures of dating a woman that one enjoyed, could
lead to a miserable marriage. Only by a careful comparison with
other of one's experiences within the general classifications
possible for the description of an experience can one tell which
properties really do make the experience valuable.

However, one should not commit the fallacy of thinking that
only one description is important for each experience, since there
may be several. I greatly enjoy conversing with Jim, and this is
so both because I enjoy talking with intelligent people with similar interests and because of the complex and unique set of characteristics that Jim has. Thus I might decide from these experiences
with Jim to seek activities which involve conversation with people
of similar interests(whoever they may be) and also to develop a
closer relationship with Jim.

When one has found which kinds of experiences give him pleasure, he should then evaluate them as to the degree to which they
satisfy him and, if he has had a series of a kind of experience,
diagnose that history to see if he is finding the activity more
or less satisfying as he matures. What kind of activities have
satisfied one most fully? What contexts have become more stimulating and pleasureful? Which less? If a person can answer these
questions well, he will then know which of the activities he has
already experienced will continue to give him pleasure.

However, taking an inventory of what experiences have pleased
one is not an adequate basis for choosing activities, for some
pleasureful contexts might lead to unfortunate and painful experiences or might have been replaced by even more pleasing activities.
For instance, many people find watching television to be a pleasant
activity, but decide not to watch it because they feel they would
receive more enjoyment from other activities like reading books or
conversing with friends, activities which, unlike most television
watching, can lead to other intrinsically valuable experiences.
We have already seen in the example of Joe and his elegant home
how a pleasing experience could not be made into a value because
the consequences were disastrous, and everyone's life is filled
with examples of pleasures rejected because the means cost too
much. I would love to have a sports car and can afford it, but
this would mean that I could not also afford to travel, eat well,
entertain friends, or buy books, and as these latter activities
are all more valuable than the pleasures from having a sports car,
this possibility is rejected. The importance of grasping what

means are necessary for an activity, what the consequences of that activity are, and what else one might do in place of that activity cannot be overstressed. The calamities which are caused by the failure of people to understand the relations between their activities is at the heart of the downfall of Oedipus and is the substance of many other tragedies. We seek what we believe to be in our good, but do not grasp what its full issue will be, and thereby reap suffering rather than satisfaction.

There is one aspect of these interconnections of activities to which a person should pay special attention, namely, the general conditions which must prevail in order for one to have almost any attainment of pleasure at all. These conditions often do not cause satisfactions directly but rather allow them to happen. My health did not cause me to enjoy hiking, but without it I never would have had that pleasure. Although these general conditions can vary in number and degree from person to person, most people need to have good health, food, protection from painful climatic conditions, and security from fear of injury and/or violent death. Without some kind of minimal securing of these conditions very few people can experience many kinds of enjoyments, and, thus, it is important in one's reasoning about values to give utmost priority to the securing of these conditions whenever there is any doubt about them.

Now, with this accumulated knowledge of which contexts have given him the most satisfying experiences, whether those contexts are rising or declining in their abilities to satisfy him, what means are necessary to produce the experiences and what consequences those activities will have on future satisfactions, the agent is in a strong position to predict which of the activities he has already experienced should be pursued in order to achieve the most satisfaction. Although all of this sounds terribly complicated, it is basically what we do every day in a more or less haphazard way. We tend to repeat those activities which have given us pleasure and which we feel do not cost too much either in means or consequences, and we avoid those activities which we think do cost too much or which eventually caused us more pain than we thought them worth. All the above has attempted to do is to make these methods explicit and urge a more rigorous application of them than is usually given.

However, these procedures leave one vital question unanswered: how should one decide which as yet unexperienced contexts to enter? This is a significant problem because many of the most crucial decisions we make concern such contexts: Should I marry Joan? Should I become a teacher of philosophy? Should we have a child? It is obvious that the method of "try it and see if you like it" will not do for the most important of these contexts, in that they often involve serious commitments which cannot be easily broken or undone. If one has no experience in these activities, how is he to decide which of them will provide him with a maximum of pleasure?

The first step one should take in determining what new contexts to pursue is to discern what activities are available to him within his environment. Then, when one is aware of those possibilities, he can use several forms of analogical reasoning to calculate which of them will probably be pleasureful for him. One, a person can predict which of these possibilities will probably give him the most pleasure by finding which of them are similar to the activities that have been most satisfying to him in the past. Second, a person can predict what new contexts will be valuable for him by seeing what people similar to him in desires, character, and abilities have found satisfying in their lives. This seeking of advice from others (either through books, other media, or personal acquaintance), who one thinks have similar characters to his own, is very important. If a person had to rely only on his own individual experiences, he would probably be in an ignorant and constantly precarious position most of the time. But since most men are similar to one another in many important ways, we can justifiably draw upon the wisdom of our friends, elders, and ancestors. However, circumstances change and people always differ from one another in some respects; what worked for one person or society need not be appropriate for another. The only way of evaluating which former solutions should be accepted is by seeing why the satisfactions occurred and whether the present conditions are similar to those which were responsible for the earlier successes.

Let me illustrate these methods of choosing pleasureful contexts with an extended example. Imagine a young man in the middle of his college years attempting to decide what kind of profession to pursue, and assume that he has already decided that what he really values are pleasureful activities. From examining his recent life he has found that the following contexts have given him the most pleasure: recreational non-competitive outdoor activities (hiking, skiing, swimming, etc.), reading and discussing literature, philosophy, religion, and politics (but literature the most), and activities in which he sets his own pace and standards rather than those in which what he does is controlled by others. He also gets a modest satisfaction from having nice clothes, being in well-furnished homes, and eating good food. But above all he gets pleasure from conversing and interacting with people, especially when the conversation is focused on ideas concerning the human condition.

When he comes to analyze his character traits he decides

41

that he is quite friendly and congenial but not dynamic or forceful either in making friends or presenting himself to others. He
is very sensitive to the beauties of nature and art and the desires
and needs of other people. He also discovers that he is not very
disciplined and cannot stay with a demanding task for long. Finally, he finds himself to be non-competitive with a tendency to
become very anxious when having to match his talents against those
of others. His abilities or lack of them, as one might suspect,
fit the picture already given: he has physical strength and stam-
ina, a fine facility in communicating with others, and, except in
mathematical and scientific subjects, good reasoning skills in
both practical and ideational affairs.

He now looks for what profession will most satisfy him and
concludes after an initial analysis that nothing seems better than
being a college professor of literature, for such a job involves
interacting with other people on humanistic ideas, allows one
great personal control over what and how he teaches, gives a salary high enough to satisfy his modest material desires, appears
relatively non-competitive, and has lengthy periods of vacations
during which time he would be free to enjoy outdoor recreational
activities. To test this hypothesis he decides to ask those pro-
fessors who he thinks are most like him (informal, sensitive,
congenial) what being a professor is like and what it requires.
He elicits that far from being non-competitive, the academic world
is often brutally competitive and that to survive in it one must
often make the student-teacher relationship secondary to publish-
ing and research. Also, at least one well-documented and detailed
thesis is required for the Ph.D. and to complete this demands an
extraordinary amount of discipline. Our student now realizes that
he is probably not well-suited for the world of college academics.
He then looks into being a forest ranger, but while this would
satisfy his love of outdoor activity and give him much independ-
ence, he fears that there would not be sufficient opportunities
to satisfy his desires for the cultural interactions that he
loves. Social work appeals to him in that it essentially involves personal interaction with others, but having to follow the
maze of government requirements and having to be more forceful in
human relations than he wishes to be make him reject this possibility. Finally, he writes to an older friend whom he considers
akin to him in character to inquire what challenges, frustrations,
and satisfactions he has found teaching English in high school.
When his friend writes back that he has found satisfactions beyond what he expected and that there was not a great deal of com-
petition once a job was obtained, then this appears to our student to have all the advantages of college teaching without its
major drawbacks vis-à-vis his character and abilities. But how
would he feel about interacting with teen-agers, many of whom
won't care at all for literature? Would he be too frustrated if
they could not learn what he taught them? He is not sure, for

he has never had this kind of experience, and so writes his friend inquiring into this problem and visits local high schools to observe what happens in English classes. The information he receives from these explorations is not all rosy, but the men whom he discerns as being most similar to himself all say that this problem can be a great personal challenge with as many significant rewards as failures. And, thus, our student begins to enroll in teacher training courses.

Obviously, this example, lengthy as it is, is still vastly oversimplified, especially in its isolation from other problems, such as whether, whom, or what kind of woman he wants to marry. Nonetheless, it shows what kind of reasoning can be helpful in solving problems concerning unexperienced contexts.

In summary, if a person wants to be able to predict as best he can what kinds of activities will give him the maximum of pleasure, then he must engage in a lengthy reflection in which he first attempts to determine which activities (both experienced and unexperienced) are most likely to give the maximum satisfaction. Second, he should attempt to formulate what the interconnections of these contexts are likely to be, so that he can tell to what extent these activities will tend to support or negate one another. Then on the basis of this knowledge he should choose which activities he thinks will maximally actuate the kinds of pleasures he wants and those means which will most expediently produce them.

3.3 Reasoning concerned with what will give one happiness differs significantly from reasoning dealing with pleasure in that, presumably, those who have chosen happiness have also chosen some kind of ideal by which to direct their lives. It is this ideal that is the criterion for the selection or rejection of concrete activities rather than pleasure. Does an activity help achieve the ideal, hinder it, or is it indifferent to it? It might seem that these would be fairly easy questions to answer once a definite ideal is given, for all that needs to be done is to find sub-classes of the type of experience held to be ideal. However, as will be seen, formidable problems arise in these matters.

Since one's ideal is to apply to most of his major activities and is supposedly derived from some very general and comprehensive drive, it will more than likely be expressed in a general and abstract way: e.g., "Realize yourself." "Develop yourself to the fullest." "Seek beauty." "Help others." "Be moral." "Gain wisdom." "Be creative." The great problem with these general formulations of ideals is that they suffer from a large degree of vagueness; that is, there are a number of instances in which one cannot tell if the activity in question fulfills the ideal or not. Are playing football, being a bachelor, and studying turtles instances of realizing oneself? seeking beauty?

gaining wisdom? One cannot tell without more definite concepts of 'self-realization,' 'beauty,' and 'wisdom' than are ordinarily associated with the use of these terms. Unless one develops these more precise and definite meanings for the key concepts of his ideal, it will be mere verbal decoration, unable to affect his choices and actions.

In order to clarify the concepts of one's ideal a person needs to designate what the experiential properties are in virtue of which those concepts can be predicated of activities or persons.[2] This is necessary because the key words in ideals like 'seek beauty,' 'realize oneself,' and 'always be moral' are what are known as consequential property words--words that do not refer to an experienced property but which are asserted of an activity, state of affairs, person, etc., in consequence of their having certain experientially ascertainable properties. For example, I call Ed a big man not because he has some mysterious property 'bigness' in him, but in consequence of the facts that he is over six feet tall and weighs over two hundred pounds. Designating what the experiential properties are in virtue of which one's ideal is to be asserted can be extremely difficult, for many of the concepts in ideals are levels removed from the properties of concrete experiences. For instance, 'seeking beauty' could be reduced to 'seeking experiences in which intensity of feeling arises out of harmonious contrasts between the parts of the experience.' But 'harmonious contrast' is still a consequential property term and needs to be further explicated. This one might do by saying that the parts of an experience are in a harmonious contrast if they differ significantly from each other, each is attractive in itself, and all are experienced as integral parts of a unified whole. Although this still needs further clarification of the consequential terms 'attractive' and 'unified whole,' one can see how much more direction than 'seek beauty' is given by 'seek activities which cause an intensity of feeling to arise from the experiencing of elements which are different from one another, attractive in themselves, and capable of being grasped in a unified whole.' I have never experienced the property 'beauty' and do not know how to find it, but I have had intense experiences of harmonious contrasts and these experiences can serve as a basis for finding other kinds of activities to pursue in order to fulfill the ideal of seeking beauty.

Once the concepts of an ideal are made more precise, then it will turn out to be one of two kinds: a substantial ideal or a formal one. By 'substantial ideal' I mean one which has as its

---

[2]The other techniques that can be used to clarify vague concepts are too numerous and complex to elucidate here. I recommend John Wilson's Thinking with Concepts as very helpful in this field.

essence the engaging in a specific or determinate contextual activity, such as contemplation for Aristotle, or the intellectual love of God for Spinoza. A 'formal ideal,' on the other hand, is one which does not prescribe any one definite kind of activity as good, but rather gives the conditions, which if present in any experience or activity, will make it good. For example, if one's ideal is to have aesthetic experiences in which a height of intensity is achieved through the harmonious contrast of the elements in the experience, then these conditions might be fulfilled in any number of activities--fishing, seeing a Rembrandt, studying turtles, playing with a child. No one particular kind of activity is prescribed as ideal, rather any activity can become ideal if it has the proper form.

With the demise of teleological biology and the rise to dominance of democratic principles, substantial ideals are in little favor today. It is felt that anybody in any walk of life should be able to reach an ideal and that if some men are unable to participate in the prescribed activity of a substantial ideal due to a lack of native ability or adverse economic and social conditions, this does not mean that there is something wrong with them; rather, something is wrong with the ideal. Thus, most modern ideals of excellence are of the formal kind: they do not tell one specifically what he must do, but indicate what form his experiences or character must have in order for them to be valuable. Sartre's authentic man, Nietzsche's creator of values, Whitehead's seeker of beauty, Dewey's pragmatic man having consummatory experiences, and Jung's emotionally balanced person are all examples of ideals capable of being realized by anybody doing almost anything, for it is not what is experienced but how one experiences that counts. Not only do these ideals allow many kinds of contexts to be valuable, they also are open-ended in maintaining that there is not one final and ultimate kind of experience which completely fulfills and terminates the ideal. Man is conceived as a process which has no final goal or terminus; he can become increasingly authentic, creative, pragmatic, etc. but can never exhaust his potentialities in these areas completely.

If a substantial ideal is held, then one already knows what kind of definite activity will bring him happiness (e.g., contemplation, love of God), and his primary endeavor will be to determine what he must do in order to be able to engage maximally in that activity. To do this one can use the same methods as discussed for determining what will give a person pleasure with the difference that now one will use them to discover how best to actuate the kind of activity he holds to be ideal. Formal ideals, because of their openness, are much more complex to work with than substantial ideals. Since there may be many kinds of experiences which will fulfill the ideal, a person needs to explore which of them will be best for him. Will one fulfill his ideal of self-realization best by becoming a hermit, a politician or a lens-grinder? There are no correct or incorrect general answers to questions like this, for the same activities can affect different people differently. They must be answered on the basis of each person's individual experiences, character, and abilities.

Basically, the methods for determining which activities will fulfill one's formal ideal are also those for finding what gives one pleasure with the one major change that one is now looking for activities that will have the properties prescribed by his ideal rather than the characteristic of 'giving pleasure.' As with pleasure, the proper place to begin is with an inventory of those activities which one has already experienced as having fulfilled his ideal. Again one must compare and contrast his experiences in order to isolate the critical properties which enabled the remembered experiences to satisfy the ideal. Then an analysis must be made of what means were necessary to produce the activities and what consequences they had. Were the means themselves experiences which fulfilled the ideal or were they ones which did not? Did the activity lead one to further fulfilling experiences or to ones detrimental to the ideal? Once the inventoried activities are understood in all their relations, one must then try to imagine what other experiences he might have had if he had used his time and resources differently. Could he have had even more fulfilling experiences? Answers to these questions should then give a person a firm basis on which to predict which of the contexts he has already experienced as satisfying his ideal will continue to do so.

As with pleasure, however, there still remains the important question of how one is to determine which as yet unexperienced activities will satisfy his ideal. Once again this can be accomplished both by reasoning analogically from the activities which one has already experienced as fulfilling his ideal to similar, but as yet unexperienced, contexts, and by seeing what experiences other men similar to oneself in ideal, character, and skills have found valuable. As before, one must have knowledge of the possibilities his environment offers to him and of his fulfillments, character, and abilities to engage adequately in this kind of reasoning, for the soundness of the analogical thinking will depend in each case on the number and importance of the similarities one is able to establish between what he knows about himself and his experiences and what he knows about other people and other possible experiences.

Hence, in order to determine which set of activities will give one happiness, a person must first conceptually clarify the key concepts of his ideal. Then, if the ideal is a substantial one--one which is based upon the person's being engaged in a particular activity--he needs to ascertain what resources and actions are necessary in order to put him into a position to participate in that activity. If the ideal is formal, then he needs to discover both what determinate activities have the properties prescribed by the ideal and what means are necessary to produce these. In either case, a person needs knowledge of his experiences, dispositions, and abilities, an awareness of the possibilities open to him, and an understanding of the relations of his acts and experiences to one another in order to ground adequately his decisions of what contexts to seek and what actions to take in his quest to maximally fulfill his ideal and thereby attain happiness.

3.4 As the attainment of joy involves methods already developed for dealing with pleasure and happiness, the following analysis will be merely summary. Having joy as one's end is like having a substantial ideal in that one definite kind of experience is held as valuable rather than many kinds of experiences, as is possible when one has a formal ideal or pleasure for one's end. As such, what one needs to find in seeking joy is the best way to produce this experience. Either one of two cases will be true concerning joy: a person will have already experienced it by the time he chooses it as his end or he will not have. If he already has, then his major endeavor will be to examine his experiences to determine what means were used to generate the experience, what the other consequences of this series of experiences were, and imagine whether there might be some other more effective way to evoke in him the experience of joy. If a person has not experienced joy or finds that his old methods for having this experience are no longer effective, then his principal problem will be to discover what means will most effectively produce the experience in him. In order to solve this problem he will first need to know what are the major ways other men have used to experience joy and attempt to determine which will be most effective for a man of his background and beliefs. Since these ways are almost always closely tied to certain metaphysical beliefs about the nature of the self and of the universe, the person seeking joy should also determine which of these metaphysics is closest to what he thinks is true. This, of course, raises the question of how one can tell (if he can tell at all) what metaphysical beliefs are better than others. While this is an extremely interesting and important problem, it is far beyond the scope of this work to attempt such an analysis.[3] All that needs to be said at this point is that if one does undertake an inquiry into metaphysics, then at least part of his testing of the categories in question must be an analysis of his own experiences and self, as these provide the crucial test for the general categories which are supposed

---

[3]See Whitehead's Process and Reality, Ch. 1, and Stephen Pepper's World Hypotheses, Part 1, for some interesting answers to this question.

to hold for all experiences and events. Thus, as in reasoning concerning pleasure and happiness, that concerning the attainment of joy also demands that a person come to know himself in a thorough and complete way and to understand the world insofar as it is needed to provide the means by which joy is to be experienced.

3.5 This chapter has attempted to elucidate the methods one should use in order to discover what he must do to attain the kind of experience he esteems as the most valuable. While many people use most of these procedures in a more or less casual way in their everyday lives, what is needed to be seriously prudential is a thorough and rigorous application of them. This is, indeed, a formidable task, as it involves gaining knowledge of one's self in terms of his satisfaction, character, and abilities, and an awareness of the world insofar as it provides the means for and is the locus of many of the connections of one's activities. An active imagination is also required so that one can think about what he might have done instead of what he did do, what he will probably be like in the future, and what kinds of experiences he will have in activities which he has not yet entered. Finally, his knowledge and his imagination will do him little good if his powers of reasoning are not coherent and logical, for the data he must hold in his mind and the operations he must perform on them are very complex.

Not only are all these matters arduous, but they are also unending processes. One must continue to use these procedures throughout his lifetime because he and the world are changing, often in unforeseeable ways. Means that once were easy to obtain become quite difficult to get; possibilities unavailable before become live and significant options. What once satisfied one no longer does, and what was thought abhorrent before now becomes a prized goal. Thus, not only must one engage in a major reflective examination of himself and his world, but he also must be constantly re-examining these concepts and adjusting his predictions of what will best attain the end he seeks, as he and the world change.

At this point, one will probably feel overwhelmed at the Herculean task that is being set forth. To be able to accomplish this exploration fully and adequately may well be beyond the limits of anyone's abilities. This, however, should not make us despair, for even though we may be unable to solve this problem fully, we can, nonetheless, gain various degrees of insight into ourselves, our world, and what really is in our interests. The more we grow in our awareness of ourselves and the world, the more we will be able to control whether our lives will attain a fullness of satisfaction. This reflective exploration may be immensely difficult, but the alternatives to it leave one in a very precarious position, for if a person does not have a full conception of his life, then he will be much more at the mercy of both his immediate desires, the satisfaction of which can be destructive of his greater interests, and the social and natural forces of his environment. For those who seek some kind of self-determination and autonomy there is no other choice than to commit extended periods of time and resources to the examination and exploration of one's experiences, dispositions, abilities, and the world in which he lives.

CHAPTER 4

THE PRUDENTIAL PERSON

4.1 What the last two chapters have, it is hoped, shown is
that the prudential point of view is far from what it is sometimes taken to be: simply doing what one feels like doing.
Rather, the prudential stance demands that one base his judgments
about what is in his best interests only on the objective conditions and facts that he has ascertained in a rigorous and thorough examination of himself and the world in which he lives. If
this is so, then it can be asked whether it is possible for anybody, regardless of his skills and dispositions, to take the prudential point of view, or do the methods for determining what is
in one's best interests require him to have certain particular
abilities and traits in order to perform them adequately? Although the methods for discovering what activities will satisfy
one were found to differ depending upon what end a person held to
be the most valuable; nonetheless, all of them required one to
develop at least three kinds of reasoning skills: an ability to
discern facts, an ability to use one's imagination, and an ability
to reason logically.

First, a person must be able to ascertain facts about himself and the world in which he lives insofar as they are relevant
to his attaining satisfactions. Learning these facts is a very
complicated affair, for often much more is required than just
"looking and seeing." For instance, in order to find what kinds
of experience satisfy one, a person not only needs to remember
what individual activities he has experienced as satisfying, but
also needs to abstract from them the general properties which
caused him to feel satisfaction, for without these properties no
practical generalizations about future goods can be made. The
same problems are true for finding what dispositions and skills
one has: he must examine a large number of experiences and
through comparative analysis draw from them generalizations about
the ways in which he does and can deal with the world.

Another area in which finding facts is vital but difficult
is in understanding the means to and consequences of one's activities, for in order to do this one must be able to grasp causal
connections that are oft times not very apparent and which can
demand that one gain a general knowledge of how human beings act
and react. For example, think of all one must know about himself
and human reactions in order to see the comparatively simple
connection between his generous accounts of his accomplishments and

the fact that he is rarely befriended by others. Perhaps, as complicated as any of these fact-finding processes is recognizing that a context represents a live possibility for oneself. To see this, one must have a knowledge of what is done in the context, what skills are demanded by it, to what kind of person these activities are likely to give satisfaction, and then see to what extent his own abilities and history of satisfactions fit those of the context.

It is difficult to conceive of someone's ascertaining any of these important kinds of facts unless he has developed abilities to abstract general properties from comparatively analyzed experiences, to interrelate facts about himself and the various activities open to him, and to grasp certain general truths about how the world and human beings work. All of these skills require a great deal of time and practice to develop, but until one does, he will not be able to ascertain what is in his best interests.

Secondly, the prudential person must develop skills of imaginative reasoning. The imagination demanded by practical reasoning is different from fact-finding in that it deals with what is not the case rather than with what is the case. Yet since its ultimate aim is accurate predictions, imagination must be closely tied to knowledge of the facts, especially facts concerning the causal interrelations of experiences and how people change, for without this kind of knowledge imagination will become fantasy and have either no relevance or a destructive effect on one's reasoning about what will satisfy him. For instance, in order for one to evaluate the worth of past satisfactions, he must attempt to imagine if he could have had even more satisfying experiences had he used his time and resources differently. If these imagined projections are not based upon what, in fact, are one's capacities, resources, and worldly possibilities, then his evaluation will probably be inaccurate and misleading.

Along with being a tool in evaluating past satisfactions and actions, imaginative reasoning has also been seen to play several important roles in the prediction of what kinds of future experiences will give one a maximum of satisfaction. First, a person must be able to imagine accurately what the consequences of his actions will be, for without this data he will not know whether his acts are really in his best interests or not. Also, in order to decide which general courses of action to take, one must be able to imagine both how he will probably change in the future and how that future self will probably experience the various possible contexts open to it. Crucial to one's ability to perform all of these operations is the development of a capacity to imagine how people with different wants, desires, dispositions, and abilities feel and respond in various contexts. This is necessary in order for a person both to predict the consequences of many of his actions, as these often involve other people's reacting to things he has done, and to make decisions about which long-term or future contexts to choose. Knowledge about how 'other' people feel is needed for these latter kinds of decisions, because they must be based not on how a person with his present desires would feel but on how he with his future wants and needs will probably feel: that is, how he as a different person will feel. For example, a young woman might have little desire to become a mother and very few of the dispositions needed to be a good parent. If she bases her decision of whether or not to direct her life toward the eventual having of a family only on who she is now, then her decision will be negative; but if she attempts to imagine how she will change and what this different person will want, then she might very well decide differently. How can one imagine how he will change and how that changed person will feel? Perhaps the best way is to find older people, who one thinks were like him when they were young, and attempt to determine how they changed and what gives them satisfaction.

The third ability needed in order for one to determine what end he ought to seek and how best to fulfill that end is logical thinking. Aside from the usual meaning of arguing validly from one's premises to his conclusions, logical reasoning in the prudential context entails that one should be able to universalize his claims. That is to say, one cannot make a justified prudential claim unless he can find prescriptions which he believes have universal validity. This is so because the prudential point of view demands that one be able to indicate what factors in himself and in the world are the reasons why he thinks he ought to do x, and this is equivalent to saying that any person with the same characteristics in a world with similar possibilities also ought to do x. For instance, if I say that I ought to spend at least several weeks a year hiking and camping in the mountains with my family and/or friends because I have found that these activities fulfill my ideal by giving me intense and harmonious experiences, because I am a careful and knowledgeable camper and thus these experiences will probably not lead to ruinous consequences but rather to further fulfillments in heightened friendships and sensitivities, and because the resources needed (transportation, equipment, etc.) are quite minimal and will not significantly hinder achieving other goals, then I am also claiming that anyone who discovers hiking and camping to fulfill his ideal, who is a careful and knowledgeable camper, and for whom the resources required for these activities are minimal, ought, if it is possible, to spend at least several weeks a year hiking and camping. Once one requires reasons for choosing what he does, then by the very nature of the process of giving reasons, he must commit himself to finding propositions that he can universalize as correct in all similar cases. One is free to choose from many ways of life, but this freedom is worthless unless the choice is grounded in reasons. Thus, we have the paradoxical result that in seeking what is good solely for oneself, a person must find prescriptions which he believes to have universal validity.

This criterion of universalization holds not only for prudence, but also, as R. M. Hare has shown, for all 'ought' prescriptions or value judgments. That is, whenever one says that 'x is good' or 'x ought to be done' it implies that he can indicate what the relevant characteristics of x are in virtue of which he is claiming it to be good and commits himself to making the same value judgment or prescription whenever those properties occur again. The reason why one must do this, Hare claims, is that if he doesn't he will be guilty of linguistic inconsistency, for in essence he will be saying both that certain characteristics require the application of the word 'good' and that they don't. The criterion of universalization necessitates that one be consistent in the value judgments he makes.

However, in order for a person to universalize a judgment he must be more than merely consistent, for consistency can be equivalent to blind stubbornness. Holding a belief consistently should be valued only when that belief is the product of a rational inquiry. The kind of rational examination required for a prescription to be universalized properly will depend upon the point of view from which the prescription is being made, for the rules and procedures for making value judgments in economics, physics, politics, cooking, prudence, morals, etc., are all to some degree dependent upon the differing subject-matters and goals of these fields. Thus, while the rule that all 'ought' judgments must be consistently held does not vary from context to context, the conditions under which these judgments will be said to be properly universalized are dependent on the rules of each field.

The kind of rational inquiry required by the prudential point of view for issuing universalized claims has already been delineated. It consists of those processes by which one is to determine what general end to seek, what determinate activities best fulfill that end, and what means are necessary in order to produce those activities. Thus, when it is said that one of the abilities needed to be prudential is logical thinking, what is most fundamentally meant is that a person be able to perform all those processes, synthesize the information gathered from them, and then, on the basis of this information, make value judgments to which he is willing to adhere consistently. It can be seen that what the requirement of universalization in prudence does is to prevent a person from oversimplifying his judgments. If one is tempted to say "I should watch the football game on T.V. because I feel like it," the criterion of universalization asks him if he can think of any cases in which he ought not to do something even though he feels like doing it. If there are such cases (and even the slightest amount of prudential reasoning will show that there are), then he must find a more complete reason if he wishes to justify prudentially his choice to watch the game on T.V. This demand for a 'more complete reason' will probably not be satisfied until a person can relate the activity in question to an entire conception of himself and his life. While most people are able to hold beliefs in a thoughtless but consistent way and can give some kind of reason as to why they make the value judgments they do ("I like it," "It's good for one's health," "It's what my mother did," etc.), it is a rare person who can support his universalized prudential prescriptions by reference to a unified image of his life which has been constructed from knowledge of his desires, abilities, and traits, an understanding of how acts and experiences are causally interrelated, a grasp of the possibilities open to him in the world, and a comprehension of how he will change as he matures. The ability to think like this is not something that just anyone can do at any time; it is an art which often requires years of development and practice before one can even begin to gain grounded insights into what really is in his best interests.

4.2 The last section attempted to show that one could not perform the operations demanded by the prudential point of view without developing the abilities of factual investigation, imagination, and logical reasoning. However, there are still further conditions which must be met in order to take the prudential stance, for the attainment and use of these skills requires that one also have certain dispositions. By 'disposition' or 'character trait' will be meant a general and enduring way of how a person thinks, experiences, or acts. Abilities are capacities for thinking or doing; dispositions are how the person thinks or acts. For example, someone might exercise his ability to teach children in a cheerful way, or autocratic way, or loving way, etc., and these 'ways' will represent dispositions of that person. Abilities and character traits both differ from constantly changing individual thoughts, experiences, and sensations in that they tend to be enduring and difficult to alter. They, perhaps more than any other factors, represent the continuing identity of a person. Although there are probably many dispositions needed to reason prudentially, it is at least necessary for a person to develop the following four: objectivity, impartiality, thoroughness or rigor, and sensitivity.

By the trait of 'objectivity' or 'being objective' will be meant having a disposition (a) not to let one's emotions or preconceived notions distort the facts and (b) to make one's decisions on the basis of reasons rather than on the strength of his temporary emotions. This does not mean that a person must be emotionless in gathering facts or making decisions--this is quite impossible--it only means that he should not allow his inquiries or decisions to be affected by those kinds of passions which can either make him misjudge the facts or evoke a hasty decision which is not in his best interests. This is an important trait for the prudential person to have, for too often in our quests to discover facts or imagine real possibilities we are so intent on finding what we want to find that we distort the facts to fit our preconceived pictures. This is especially true of self-analyses in which one often has a strong bias toward discovering abilities and traits that are either societally praised or ones he admires, but which he very well might not have. As Nietzsche, in his characteristic way, asks: "What is most difficult? . . . Stepping into filthy waters when they are the waters of truth, and not repulsing cold frogs and hot toads?"[1] One may be inclined not to discover and accept the "cold frogs and hot toads" of his personality and world, but unless he does, his prudential reasoning will have an erroneous base and, depending on the importance of the misjudged facts, could lead to more or less catastrophic consequences. From this and the previous illustrations of how basing one's choices on temporary emotions rather than rational inquiry can be ruinous, it should be evident that one can't adequately exercise the fact-finding and imaginative procedures of prudence unless he has the disposition of being objective.

The trait of 'impartiality' is the disposition to treat like things alike, or not to treat two things differently unless one can find a relevant reason for distinguishing between them. The prudential person must develop this trait of being impartial, for without it, he will not be able to make value judgments rationally. If one says that x is good and y is not good but is unable to indicate a significant difference between x and y, then he is violating the principle of universalizability and is being inconsistent. Certainly, if one starts making inconsistent judgments, he will have very little chance of coherently directing his life so as to attain what is in his interests. But does impartiality also mean that one cannot favor his interest over anyone else's? If this is so, then it seems a contradiction of the prudential point of view. The answer is that so long as one remains in the prudential stance, what counts as a relevant reason for distinguishing between acts or things is that one will aid or hinder his interests more or less than the other. To find that action x aids one's interests more than y is both a relevant reason for distinguishing x from y and choosing x. Impartiality as a trait of character means only that one is disposed to finding reasons for making differing value judgments; as such it has nothing to do with determining what the criteria for the reasons should be. That is a matter to be decided by the rules of the point of view in which the judgment is being made.

It has also been shown that in order to think prudentially

---

[1]Friedrich Nietzsche, Thus Spoke Zarathustra, p. 26, Viking Press.

a person must reason through practical problems as completely as possible. He must attempt to see all the major possibilities of action open to him, understand the means necessary to achieve them, and, on the basis of the knowledge he has gained about himself and the possible activities, predict the consequences of each of them on his interests. It is very doubtful that someone will be able to do this without having a disposition to be thorough and rigorous in his thinking. The prudential person cannot be inclined to accept the usual or first solution to a serious practical problem; rather his character will demand that it be carefully and completely thought through. This trait of being thorough is not easily engendered, for human beings in the main seem disposed to making hasty and facile judgments in order to rid themselves of the tensions caused by being in problematical situations, but unless one does develop this rigorous way of dealing with problems, then it is doubtful that his decisions will be in his best interests.

Finally, the prudential person needs to be a sensitive human being. By 'sensitive' is meant a disposition to be aware of those wants and needs that are often hidden and complex in oneself and in others. Why a person needs to be sensitive to his own deepest wants and desires needs no explanation, but why should he be sensitive to others? There are several reasons for this. One, other people are often the medium by which one's acts have effects on his future experiences, and unless one is sensitive to how they feel he can miscalculate what effects his acts will have. For instance, suppose I want Beth to love me and attempt to bring this state of emotion about by forcing her to embrace me on the supposition that all women want domineering men. If Beth is a person who resents being dominated and needs to interact with someone on an equal basis in a gentle way, then I will not reap the consequences I want. Secondly, a person can learn a great deal about himself by being sensitive to others. It has been shown that one of the main techniques for predicting both how one is going to change and what long-term or future contexts will bring a person satisfaction is to find other people similar to oneself and learn from them how they changed and what gives them satisfaction. One can determine if another person is similar to himself only if he is sensitive to the wants and needs of that other person. However, it should be noted  in order not to be misleading, that the disposition of being sensitive to the needs of others does not necessarily imply that one must be responsive to them. Whether and how one ought to respond to these needs will depend upon the circumstances and consequences of the situation and the point of view that one takes in acting.

4.3 Hopefully, the foregoing analysis will dispel the oft-held but erroneous portrait of the self-seeking person as a single-minded tyrant bent on satisfying some crass drive, insensitive to finer emotions in himself and in other people. He is also often seen as shallow, out of touch with the most fundamental of human emotions and concerned mainly with the immediate satisfaction of his every whim regardless of its consequences. As opposed to this view, the one offered here demands that the person who seeks his own good be an objective, impartial, and sensitive person who is keenly aware of his emotions and able to base his decisions on the most thorough and rigorous of inquiries. He must have these abilities and dispositions not because prudential reasoning finds them to be inherently worthwhile, but because he could not rationally discover anything worthwhile without them. That is, these traits might not be needed for a person to experience satisfaction, but they are necessary if he is to determine for himself what will best give him satisfaction.

This picture of the prudential person is quite similar to the classical Greek view of the ethical man as one whose appetites are ruled by his reason. Both this position and the Greeks maintain that reason should control the desires not because they are bad and need to be subverted or negated, but because desires are atomistic, bent on their individual satisfactions, and are thus unable to take the good of the person as a whole into account. Indeed, the very reason why appetites must be ruled by intelligent thought is that this is the only way to satisfy them as fully as possible. Thus, reason is not conceived of as some self-contained faculty apart from the desires with its own special ends; rather, it is a tool which man has developed in order to aid him in satisfying his desires. We reason not to stifle satisfactions, but to maximize them.

Also, as in the philosophies of Plato and Aristotle, the claim is made here that in order for one to be able to direct his desires so as to achieve what is in his interests, he must develop certain abilities and dispositions. These are what the Greek called aretai: traits which one must have if he is going to function well. As the soldier cannot defend well without courage nor the athlete compete well without strength, so the prudential man cannot accomplish his task of finding what is in his interests without being imaginative, logical, objective, impartial, thorough, and sensitive to the needs and wants of himself and others. To develop these aretai is to give oneself a lasting character with which he can control the strength of his immediate passions and aim his actions at what is truly in his best interests.

Now, the criticism might be raised that what seems to be set forth here is the unjustified normative claim that the best kind of life for the prudential person is the life ruled by reason. But this has not been asserted, for I have never contended that the life of reason is best, only that one cannot determine what is in one's best interests without being rational. However, this criticism does reveal a fundamental paradox. What would happen if the conclusion of one's rational inquiry was that he should live as recklessly and unthoughtfully as possible in order to achieve the most satisfaction? Could he live this way? The problem is that a person can't change characters like a suit of clothes; once one has developed the abilities and dispositions necessary to determine rationally what is in his best interests, he cannot very easily divest himself of them.

However, difficult as it is to alter one's character, it is far from impossible, and the person who has found that he ought to be thoughtless could work at gradually losing his rational hang-ups. But this will not do, for the conditions and structure of desires which were the basis for the conclusion to live irrationally are temporarily contingent and might at any time change so as to negate the conclusion. One cannot determine at any one particular time what will always be good for him, for he must constantly be able to examine himself and the world in which he lives in order to adjust his prescriptions to fit the changes that occur.

Thus, while I have not attempted to prove that the life directed by reason is the best way to gain a maximum of satisfaction, it turns out that once one decides to determine for himself what is in his own interest, he also commits himself to making his decisions on the basis of reason and to developing the requisite abilities and dispositions for doing so. It might possibly not be in one's best interest to become so thoughtful, but the only way to discover this is by becoming thoughtful and remaining so.

4.4 A fitting way to conclude this portrait of the prudential person is by comparing him to the artist, for a man's constructing of his life is analogous to the artist's creation of a work of art. Both need materials with which to build, skills by which to unite these into some kind of form, and lively imaginations if they are not simply to repeat what others have done. As with the works of artists, the lives produced by different individuals will be immensely varied: some will be fairly ugly and impoverished, many will only be variations of the popular style of the day, but some lives will be such masterpieces of structure and content that they, like the works of the great masters, will stand out from all the others as uniquely individual and set paradigms for what human lives can be.

In order to construct his life, the prudential person needs materials with which to build it. These materials are the various contexts or activities available to him. As with the artist, the prudential person will probably select his materials, or contexts, on the basis of which of them he feels he has some ability to manipulate successfully and/or with which he is already familiar. Depending on the range of skills he has developed, the breadth of experience he has had, and his ability to imagine how his skills might be applicable to new possibilities, a person will engage himself in fairly traditional and safe contexts, adventurously explore unusual possibilities of experience, or try some combination of both of these. The decision of which activities to attempt to incorporate into one's life is quite complex, for he can choose many of them or few, ones similar in kind or wildly diverse. Too many elements may make one's life a hodgepodge of unconnected pieces, while too few could make it monotonously dull. Diversity is to be valued, but one must be careful, for some contexts are as mutually destructive as a Picasso head would be on a Titian body. Unlike the artist who can paint over mistakes or get a new block of marble, people who are wrong in their choices of activities are often scarred by them for a lifetime. The proper choice of activities is, therefore, vital for the creation of a well-constructed life.

Selecting what activities to use in creating one's life is, however, only part of the problem and cannot be separated from the question of how to unite them into some kind of coherent form. The artist and prudential person must both discover which of their materials (activities) tend mutually to support one another and in what combination they do this best. Do some materials dominate so much that lesser constituents are lost, as decoration can hide design in art or as professionalism can make one unable to appreciate other experiences in life? Are there some materials which are extraneous, clutter the whole, and thereby detract from it? In order to solve these problems the artist and prudential person both need to find models by which to unify their materials and activities and these can come from three major sources: others, one's past, and one's imagination. Often people decide how to live by following the typical patterns of others in their societies. The kind of person or artist who does this is basically a copier, and this will be more or less adequate depending on whether one has fairly typical desires and abilities and on whether the usual patterns are satisfying to him. Secondly, one might base the pattern of his future life on what he has done and found satisfying in the past. Although this kind of model in both life and art produces repetitions and is often stagnant, it is also true that there are many kinds of art and activities that deserve to be repeated. Finally, one can attempt to construct novel patterns for integrating his activities by the use of his imagination. This can be quite dangerous, especially if one's imagination radically departs from the given models of his society and past experiences, but it is the only way that one can break the tyranny of these past habits and societal models so as to put himself in a position to be able to judge critically which kind of life will bring him the most satisfaction. Probably everyone uses all three of these sources in varying combinations with the societal model being by far the most usual and dominant.

However, it is only when one attempts to use his imagination to construct ideational pictures of possible ways he could live that he can really be free to choose for himself that pattern of life which best fits his personal desires, abilities, and circumstances. In life, as in art, it is the ability to imagine new possibilities for creation that distinguishes the great masters from the very fine craftsmen.

Will one's life be a dull copy of the popular style or will he infuse it with originality? Will it consist merely of a series of events like one sound after another, or will he orchestrate his activities into a symphonic whole? Will one be able to choose and organize his contexts so as to make his life like a fine novel or cathedral or painting: a rich diversity of elements integrated in a novel and harmonious way?

This part of the book has attempted to delineate what abilities, dispositions, and reasoning processes a person must develop if he is going to attempt to achieve some kind of autonomous control over his life and be able to construct it, as the artist constructs his work of art. They are not easily attained. Many long and painful hours of reflection and research are required, but their reward is unexceeded by that of any other activity, for it is nothing less than the person's own life.

4.5 Becoming able to determine what actions are in one's best interests is essential if one is to answer for himself the central ethical question of "How ought I to live?" But is the determination of one's interest the only problem that must be solved in order to be a fully ethical thinker? As was seen in Chapter 1, there are many philosophers who claim that it is, and many others who maintain that one cannot think or act ethically unless he is willing to take the moral point of view in all cases in which his interests conflict with those of other people. Insofar as the foregoing analysis of the prudential stance has basically been concerned with the individual's relationship with himself and not with a critical examination of his relationship with others, it has been an inadequate exploration of the ethical problem. Should the moral stance supersede the prudential, or are there no occasions on which we should act against our interests? In order to answer this question we first must examine what the moral point of view is, for only after this has been done can we attempt to discover how the moral and prudential views are related, and which one, if either, can be said to take precedence over the other.

PART II: MORALS


CHAPTER 5


WHAT DOES IT MEAN TO BE MORAL


5.1 If prudence is defined as that point of view whose
function is to determine what is in an individual's best interests, it might then be thought that morals would be defined as
that discipline whose purpose is to determine what is in the
best interests of everyone. However, although the definition for
prudence is generally accepted, the one for morals is not. Rather, what it means to be moral has been a question of extensive
philosophical debate from the time of Plato to the present day.
Some have held that being moral meant creating the greatest possible balance of good (usually identified with satisfaction,
pleasure, or happiness) over evil, while others have thought that
being moral meant following certain laws such as "Do not lie" and
"Do not break promises," regardless of whether following such
laws would produce the greatest welfare. Still others have said
that being moral meant treating all people equally, while their
opponents have protested that being moral meant always seeking
one's own advantage. Why has there been such a disputation over
what it means to be moral?

The problem is that the word 'moral' is not a simple descriptive word whose only purpose is to designate a certain language game or point of view. It is what C. L. Stevenson called
an 'emotive word,' a word which is strongly associated with pro-
attitudes and which is often primarily used to commend a person's
maxims, acts, or character. If someone calls a person moral, we
almost always understand this to be commendation of him, and if
someone is said to be immoral or amoral we would almost always
take this to be a condemnation. Because the word 'moral' has
this strong commendatory meaning, any attempt to define it in
terms of a kind of action automatically creates a normative principle. For instance, if one said that 'being moral' meant 'following the Ten Commandments,' then the normative principle "Follow the Ten Commandments" would automatically be posited. But
if this is done then the distinction between 'morals' and 'good
morals,' between 'doing what is moral' and 'doing what is morally good,' is collapsed.

While collapsing this distinction is an easy thing to do,
its consequences are disastrous, for it eliminates the concept

of 'bad morals' or 'mistaken morals' as a self-contradictory notion. If this happens, then any normative principle different from the one said to be definitive of morals must be held to be non-moral, and, thus, there can be no moral disputes or arguments because any position different from the given definition is simply not a moral one. There is no possibility of questioning the given principle within the moral framework because that principle supposedly defines what the moral framework is. Yet, morals, insofar as it is taken to be the highest prescriptive language, must always involve the possibility of disputes and of questioning any existing set of values or rules.[1] That is to say, one of the major functions of the language of morals is to allow individuals to critique the way that they are living, to critique the values of their societies, and to formulate their own values for themselves.

This is why attempts to justify any type of utilitarian theory (one ought always to create the greatest possible balance of good over evil) or deontological theory (one ought always to follow a certain set of moral laws) by saying that the theory is what it means to be moral must be inadequate. If 'being a utilitarian' were linguistically equivalent to 'being moral,' then all the deontological theories which have been so important in the history of the West (especially in Christian ethics) would not be merely mistaken moral theories, they would not be moral theories at all, and the same would be true of the utilitarian theories if a particular deontological theory were taken to be the meaning of morals. The history of morals has been a history of disputes, and these cannot be solved by one proponent saying of the others that they do not know how to use the word 'moral.' If many candidates can be presented as the best moral principles, then none of them can be simply what it means to be moral.

The impossibility of making a normative principle analytic to the concept of morals has given rise to two important non-normative positions on what it means to be moral: relativism and prescriptivism. Both of these views take the 'freedom' aspect of morals to be basic and thus maintain that no moral principle can be conclusively justified. The difference between them is that relativism will allow for no form of justification while prescriptivism advances a limited type of reasoning for the determination of moral beliefs. We must now turn to these views to see if they provide answers for the question of what it means to be moral.

5.2 Relativistic theories are not based so much on how people actually use moral language as they are on how one must view morals after he discovers that no moral maxims can ever be fully

---

[1]This is the 'freedom' aspect of morals which was dealt with at length in 1.4 and will thus be given a summary treatment here.

justified. Relativists hold that if there is no normative principle necessary to the concept of morals, then morals is not a
rational discipline, for it can provide no basis for claims made
within it. But if morals is not a rational discipline, what is
it? Although different relativists will give different answers
("morals expresses one's desires," "moral language represents
one's feelings," "morals is an emotive language by which we both
express our feelings and try to influence the feelings of others"),
most of them understand morals to be akin to the language of
taste in which each individual can express his peculiar preferen-
ces and not be subject to refutation on them.

The strength of this position is that it captures the very
important personal or individual aspect of morals. To be a moral
agent means that one must decide for himself how he is to act;
his action must be consciously willed. If one blindly and unques-
tioningly follows the dictates of the authorities of his environment then he is not really acting. No one else can make a moral
agent's decisions for him; in order to be autonomous he must give
himself his own maxims. This view of the moral agent has been
held by relativists and nonrelativists alike. However, the relativists claim that this notion makes sense only if there is no
given principle which people must follow in order to be moral.
What kind of freedom is it when one is only free to follow a
given moral principle?

Although the relativists seem to do justice to the concepts
of freedom and autonomy in morals, this is not so, for by denying
that moral decisions are rational they negate any meaningful concept of freedom or autonomy. If one's free decisions can have no
rational grounds, then choosing is equivalent to caprice, for
without some kind of basis upon which to act, all choices must be
merely arbitrary. If what the relativists say about the impossibility of reasoning in morals is true, then they cannot explain
why morals, freedom, and autonomy are so highly valued or desired,
for rather than being a stance of self-determination and action,
morals is merely letting oneself be governed by chance or whimsey.

There are other more noted problems with relativism. Many
people think that there really are right and wrong ways to act
and spend a tremendous amount of time and energy attempting to
reason through moral situations to find what they ought to do.
Should we say to all these people that they are deluded, that
reasoning can bring no answers in morals? Also, if relativism is
correct, then there really can be no moral disagreements because
there can be no principle by which disagreements can be adjudicated. Moral judgments are like those of taste: each to his own.
Yet, it seems very strange to propose that the values and actions
of the kindest and most benevolent of people cannot be said to be
any better than those of the cruelest and most dastardly of ty-
rants. Nonetheless, this is a clear consequence of a theory

which holds that there are no criteria for distinguishing correct from incorrect conduct.

"That's enough!" now retorts the relativist. "I do not propound to explicate ordinary usages of morals because, as I said, I have found that people are deluded about what the nature of morals really is. Thus, it is no criticism of my position to show that it does not correspond with how people use moral language. If you disagree with my position, then there is one and only one way by which it can be destroyed and that is by showing that there is a legitimate sense of justification in morals." He is right--this is the only way to challenge relativism, and it is a very difficult thing to do without falling into the trap of attempting to make an ultimate principle analytic to the concept of morals. The most significant recent attempt to answer this problem has come from the founder and leading exponent of prescriptivism, R. M. Hare.

5.3  Unlike the other positions already examined, Hare's prescriptivism[2] does not attempt to define morals in terms of its having or not having a normative principle necessary to its conception. Rather, he wishes to define moral language in terms of following certain methodological rules. These rules, according to Hare, do not contain any substantial principle about how people should act; they are only logical rules which must be followed if one is to use moral language in a linguistically meaningful way. In particular, there are two cardinal rules which must be followed in all uses of moral language:  (1) moral language must always be used prescriptively, and (2) all moral prescriptions must be universalized.

What is meant by saying that moral language is prescriptive is that its major purpose is to guide or direct conduct. Moral language is a practical language and its basic concern is in answering the question "What should I do?" Thus, all uses of moral language must, directly or indirectly, entail prescriptions of how one ought to act. Although some uses like "Mary is a morally good person" may not appear to prescribe any action, at least part of the meaning of this judgment is "People ought to act as Mary does." It seems nonsensical to hold both that "Mary is a morally good person" and that "No one should act like Mary." Hence, according to Hare, all moral judgments can be translated into 'ought' assertions, and every 'ought' assertion implies an imperative demanding that something be done.

---

[2]This section is not intended to be a careful and lucid analysis of Hare's philosophy, but an examination of his views in the context of the ongoing themes and structure of this book. For a more complete elucidation of Hare, I recommend W. D. Hudson's Modern Moral Philosophy, Part IV.

But is it true that all moral 'oughts' imply an imperative? What imperative is implied by "Julius Caesar ought not to have crossed the Rubicon," where this is used as a moral condemnation? One cannot give imperatives to dead men, and the sentence is not telling everybody who travels in Italy not to cross the Rubicon, so it appears that no imperative is implied.

In order to grasp how Hare would reply to this, one needs to understand another rule concerning the use of moral language: every moral evaluation implies that there are certain empirical properties in virtue of which the evaluation is made. That is, if two objects (people, acts, etc.) are empirically the same, then the evaluations of them must also be the same. The objects cannot differ only in that one has some non-natural property of 'goodness' or 'rightness' while the other does not. If Jane and Mary do exactly the same kinds of actions, one cannot say that Mary's acts are good but Jane's are not; one must be able to point to an experientially recognizable difference between their acts in order to evaluate them differently. Hence, if an evaluation of an object (person, act, etc.) is to be a genuine one, then there must be some reasons for it and these must include certain properties which the object (person, act, etc.) has. "Mary is good because she helps others," "He acted wrongly because he broke his promise." "It is good to have children because no other experience can give one more pleasure." These reasons or properties in consequence of which an evaluation is made need not be actually stated or apparent in the first-order judgment[3] (i.e., "Mary is a good person"), but one must have some idea of what they are in order for his value judgment to be meaningful.

There is one more essential step that must be accomplished if one is to make a legitimate value judgment. In order to argue from the fact that an object (person, act, etc.) has properties x to the conclusion that it is to be evaluated in a certain way, one must use a general warrant, tying x with the particular evaluation of the conclusion. For example, if I cite as reasons for calling Mary a good person the facts that she helps others and obeys the Ten Commandments, then in order to derive my evaluation from these facts, I must hold the general warrant "Anyone who helps others and obeys the Ten Commandments is a good person." Without this principle there is no logical connection between Mary's helping others and obeying the Ten Commandments and her being good. Thus, all moral judgments about particular people, acts, objects, etc., require one (a) to know what the properties are in virtue of which the claim is being made and (b) to assent to a general warrant connecting all cases of the occurrences of

---

[3]A first-order judgment is one which makes an evaluation of a particular person, act, event, etc.

of those properties with the type of evaluation asserted.

These general warrants underlying first-order moral judgments are the keys to understanding their cognitive meanings (in that they give the properties in consequence of which the evaluations are being made) and provide the basis for the imperatives implied by the first-order judgments. For example, the imperative implied by the person who judged Mary to be good because she helped others and obeyed the Ten Commandments is not "Be like Mary" (which could include many unintended acts) but "Help others and obey the Ten Commandments." To find the imperative implied by any value judgment which is not itself an assertion of a general principle, one must determine what the general warrant underlying the judgment is and then see what imperative is derived from it.

We can now solve the problem of how an imperative is implied in past value judgments like "Julius Caesar ought not to have crossed the Rubicon." Suppose the person makes this evaluation because he thinks that Caesar's act greatly disrupted the social order. In order to derive his conclusion about the wrongness of Caesar's act from this fact, he would have to hold the general principle that all acts which greatly disrupt the social order are wrong. This general warrant applies not only to past acts but also to all present and future acts and it implies the imperative: "Do not greatly disrupt the social order." Thus, while the imperatives are often not directly entailed by moral judgments about particular persons, objects, or events, every such value judgment does imply that its author can cite a general warrant connecting his evaluation to definite properties of the person, object, or event, and this general principle does directly imply an imperative about what actions ought to be done or ought not to be done.

It can now be seen why the use of moral language commits one to acting in a certain way. Every moral judgment is either an assertion of a general normative principle or else implies such a principle, and every general normative principle implies a general imperative about how people should act. The principle "Helping others is good" entails the imperative "Help others," and "Breaking promises is wrong" implies "Do not break promises." Since these prescriptions are general and supposedly hold for all men, the author of them must see his own actions as governed by them. If one considers morals to be the most authoritative prescriptive language and if his actions do not coincide with his principles, then we must say either that he is not free to act in the way he wants to (due to some exterior or psychological forces), or else that he does not sincerely hold his principles as moral ones. As Hare says, "It is a tautology to say that we cannot sincerely assent to a command addressed to ourselves, and at the same time not perform it, if now is an occasion for performing it and it is in our (physical and psychological) power for doing so."[4] Morals is a language of action; to make any moral judgment commits a person to acting in certain definite ways and his failure to act in these ways when it is in his power to do so means that he is not holding his principles as moral ones. Thus, the essential meaning of the rule that moral language should be used prescriptively is that one must be willing to direct his actions according to the moral principles he holds.

The second rule that Hare advances as necessary for the correct use of moral language is that one must be willing to universalize his moral principles. As was said before,[5] this means that if a person assigns a moral predicate to an act (person, object, etc.) because that act has a certain set of properties, then whenever those properties occur again, the same moral predicate must also be applied. For instance, if I say Richard acted wrongly because he lied, then I commit myself to calling all acts of lying wrong, even if they are my own acts and in my own interests. Although some philosophers have thought the principle of universalization to be a normative principle, Hare demonstrates that it really is only a logical principle demanding consistency of linguistic usage. The descriptive or cognitive meaning of the use of any moral predicate is that set of characteristics in virtue of which that predicate is asserted of an act (object, person, etc.), and if on one occasion a person says that moral term x is to be associated with set of properties y and on another occasion that x is not to be connected with y, then he is using the term x inconsistently. But if one is to use any language meaningfully, he must be consistent in his usage of it, and, hence, if moral language is to be used meaningfully then one must be willing to universalize his claims.

Thus, according to prescriptivism, a person is free to follow any principle he wishes, so long as he is willing to universalize it and live by it. As such, it is a form of relativism in that there can be no adjudication between people who hold conflicting principles and who are willing to universalize and prescribe them. However, Hare thinks that with the application of his rules, most moral disputes can be resolved. This is because most people have the same basic desires and would not be willing to universalize a claim which negated or arbitrarily overrode those interests. For instance, if I maintain that it is right to suppress a group because they hold beliefs different from mine, then I commit myself to the principle that anyone ought to suppress a group which holds beliefs different from his own. But this

---

[4] *Language of Morals*, p. 20.

[5] See 4.1.

principle entails that if I belong to a group which thinks differently from someone else, and he attempts to suppress me, then I must say that he is doing what he ought to do. Thus, even though I desire to see my opponents suppressed, I cannot say that this ought to be done because I could not agree to having it done to me if I were in the same position as my opponents. My desire not to be arbitrarily suppressed is far stronger than my desire to silence views opposed to mine. Because most people desire such basic things as survival, freedom from pain and injury, and freedom to pursue their interests more than any secondary desires, they cannot assent to any prescription in which these interests are destroyed or arbitrarily overridden.

Of course, there is always the possibility of someone's becoming a fanatic, a person who holds an ideal that he thinks should be advanced even if it directly entails the deaths or suffering of other people. Hare uses the example of the Nazi whose ideal involves the elimination of the Jewish people, and shows that in order for the Nazi to maintain this ideal as a moral principle, he must be willing to universalize it to the extent that he would assent to the killing of his family and himself if it were discovered that they were, unbeknownst to them, Jews. Hare believes that the number of people who can universalize their fanatical ideals so that they would willingly give up their lives or freedom if they themselves were found to be impediments to the ideal is quite small. However, if there are people willing to universalize such ideals and act according to them, then their positions must be classified as moral ones.

The strength of Hare's position is that he takes both freedom and reason in morals seriously and tries to give each aspect its due without destroying one or the other. He maintains that there are no normative principles which are known to be necessarily true or analytic to the concept of morals. Each man is, therefore, free to direct his actions according to any principles he wants. But if these principles are to be moral ones, then the person must be willing to universalize them and assent to occasions, real or imagined, in which he is the recipient of his own act rather than the doer of it. Thus, he must attempt to determine through a vigorous rational inquiry if there are any situations in which he could not assent to the action's being done if he were in the recipient's position. If there are such occasions, then he cannot sincerely universalize his maxim. So, on the one hand, Hare avoids the error of collapsing the distinction between 'morals' and 'good morals' by refusing to build into his concept of morals a normative principle. On the other hand, he avoids the complete subjectivity and capriciousness of relativism by demanding that all moral principles be universalized. Neither freedom nor reason is absolute; both require and limit each other.

Hare's view of prescriptivism has been severely attacked at many points, but the strongest of the criticims has been that he has not solved the freedom/reason antinomy correctly in that he has given too much prominence to freedom and not enough power to reason: the fanatic has the upper hand. How valid these attacks are depends on how one interprets Hare's concept of what it means to universalize a maxim, for he can be interpreted as saying either (1) that in order to universalize a claim one needs merely to maintain his principle consistently, or (2) that in order for a claim to be universalized it must not only be held consistently but also must be the product of a rational exploration in which one attempts to imagine the most difficult cases for his principle and see whether he could assent to that maxim's being followed from the viewpoint of any of the people involved as patients of the act. The following analysis will not attempt to adjudge which of these is the better interpretation of what Hare has written, but rather will discuss them vis-à-vis the general problem of defining the concept of ethical reasoning.

The two following examples might help to make the difference between these two concepts of universalization clearer.

1. A determines that one of his values is never to kill anybody and says that whenever one person kills another person, it is always wrong. Because A hasn't had a Socratic friend or taken a philosophy course, he never tries to test his principle against any kind of tough hypothetical example, and because his life is blessedly lucky he never faces a situation in which he or any one he knows is ever in any of those sticky situations of self-defense, war, etc. Whenever A hears of cases of killing in self-defense, or killing to save more lives, or killing to preserve a society, he does not spend any time imagining what the person committing the act faces or what the consequences of not committing the act would be; he simply says that the property of 'killing someone' has occurred and thus the act is wrong.

2. B believes that all acts of homosexual love are morally wrong and is espousing this principle to his Harian friend H. H wants to see if B really can universalize this principle and asks him to imagine himself as having a tremendously strong drive and love for males, that in making love with a man he feels a great sense of pleasure, fulfillment, and human communication, and that the consequences of this act are not disagreeable for anyone else. B says he imagines being such a person and experiencing such an act, but still finds it to be wrong. Upon questioning B, H suspects that even though B says he imagines being a homosexual and having this experience, at best this imagination consists of an abstract picture and is not at all an attempt at imaginative empathy.

69

Are examples 1 and 2 cases in which A and B have universalized principles? Insofar as we consider universalization to be merely a rule of consistent language usage, we would have to answer affirmatively. But if we think that universalization is also a conscious act which involves the processes of rigorously attempting to imagine the most difficult of hypothetical cases in which to affirm the principle in question and of sympathetically imagining what the patients of the act would feel, then A and B did not universalize their principles. For the sake of indolence I will use '$U_1$' to stand for the concept of universalization as only a rule of linguistic usage, and '$U_2$' to designate universalization as requiring both linguistic consistency and a conscious act of imaginative exploration.

Which of these concepts of universalization should one hold? The virtues of $U_1$ are (a) it is readily justified as a logical principle of linguistic consistency necessary in any kind of descriptive discourse (of which morals is a sub-class); and (b) it provides an easily recognizable test to see if a person is holding a moral principle--we simply look for consistency or inconsistency. The main drawbacks to $U_1$ are that it requires us to say that principles maintained in an insensitive, dogmatic, but consistent way satisfy the conditions of rationality and justification in ethics, and that there is no way to settle further a dispute between two consistently held beliefs.

What $U_2$ adds to $U_1$ is that in order to hold a principle in a moral way one must test that principle against the hardest hypothetical cases, attempting to imagine as sympathetically as possible the feelings of the patients of the act. This gives leverage against the pig-headed fanatic whom we suspect of not having performed a rigorous and imaginative exploration, for now we can say that although he consistently prescribes a principle, that principle is not as justified as it could be because it is not the product of rational inquiry. Also, if A holds a belief contradictory to B's and both A and B maintain their beliefs consistently, we still need not say that both are equally justified, for A's belief might be the product of a more thorough examination than B's in which case A's principle would be more justified.

It can be seen that the strengths and weaknesses of $U_2$ are just the reverse of those of $U_1$. The major benefits of $U_2$ are that it does not commit us to the view that a principle held in a consistent but rationally unexplored way is justified, and it allows for further adjudication between two principles held in a consistent way. But it has two serious deficits. First we no longer have a simple test for moral justification--consistency of linguistic behavior; now we must also examine the extent to which the moral claim is the product of rational inquiry. How are we to tell this? How do we know that the Nazi, who says that he can fully and sympathetically imagine what it feels like to be a Jew and still thinks Jews ought to be exterminated, is telling the truth? Criteria for knowing whether and to what extent a person has accomplished this rational investigation need to be more carefully developed if this concept is to have an effective function in moral argument and justification.

The second and more monumental problem with $U_2$ is how to justify it, for it is much more than a logical rule of linguistic consistency. It is one thing to say that one cannot rationally hold two contradictory moral principles and quite another to say that a moral principle must be the product of a rigorous and imaginative exploration. One could attempt to justify this by saying that an imaginative exploration is analytic to the concept of moral reasoning, but there are many people who would want to maintain that this is not so. For instance, many people have believed that the only kind of reasoning needed in morals is to see whether one's maxims coincided with those given by the predominant moral authority of his society (usually a religion, sometimes a secular government). Test cases, imagining how others feel, etc., are all unnecessary and can even be dangerous to this kind of moral view. This authoritarian approach to morals may be wrong, but insofar as it is meaningful to discuss, it is difficult to maintain that an imaginative exploration is analytic to the concept of moral reasoning.[6]

Thus, we are left with another dilemma concerning the nature of justification in morals. If one need only to be consistent in universalizing his claim, then we must say that the maxims held in an insensitive, narrow-minded, but consistent way are as justified as they can be. On the other hand, if we advance that certain rational processes must be followed in order to universalize a claim, we have to show why these should be followed, and this demonstration is extremely difficult without assuming some kind of normative principle.

5.4 If the survey of these positions has taught us anything, it is that the elucidation of what it means to be moral is an extremely difficult and complex task. The only point they all seem to agree on is that morals is that language which categori-

---

[6]It is not clear whether Hare holds $U_1$ or $U_2$, for in Ch. 2 of Freedom and Reason he defends $U_1$, while in 6.3 and 6.4 he refers to finding facts and processes of imagination as "necessary ingredients" of moral reasoning, which would point to a concept of $U_2$. Hare does not appear to see the conflict between these two, nor does he attempt any rigorous defense of imagination as necessary to ethical reasoning.

cally prescribes what one ought to do in his interactions with other people. While this is very helpful in distinguishing the purpose of morals from those of purely descriptive enterprises and in limiting the scope of what kinds of actions can be classified as moral, it does not tell us how we should determine what those prescriptions should be. It is here that we found the heart of the disagreement among these positions. Should one base his moral maxim on how it affects the welfare of others, whether or not it coincides with a simple law, whether or not he can universalize it, or simply on whatever he feels like doing? How should one attempt to justify his moral claims? This is the fundamental question that must be answered in order to elucidate the concept of what it means to be moral.

Although we are not yet in a position to answer this question positively, we can eliminate several kinds of answers to it. Firstly, any position which maintains that all moral maxims are to be justified by reference to a certain normative principle that is supposed to be analytic to the concept of morals is erroneous. Such theories collapse the distinction between 'morals' and 'good morals' and thereby have the unacceptable consequences of eliminating as non-moral any conflicting normative beliefs and of destroying the possibility of questioning whether the assumed moral principle really is the one which ought to govern human relationships. Secondly, extreme relativistic positions which deny the possibility of any reasoning at all in morals need to be rejected, for, as Hare has shown, what is minimally required by anyone making a moral judgment is that he know what the properties are in virtue of which he makes the judgment and be willing to hold his moral principles in a consistent way.

This seems to leave us with prescriptivism as the only viable concept of what it means to be moral. However, as we have seen, there can be various forms of prescriptivism depending upon what procedural rules one thinks are definitive of the justification process in morals. Which form of prescriptivism will give us the best account of justification in morals? The simplest type of prescriptivism (which Hare is often interpreted as advocating) is one in which the only rule of justification is that a person be willing to universalize his principles in the sense of holding them consistently $(U_1)$. $U_1$ is certainly a necessary condition for a judgment to be moral, for if someone either had no idea of the properties in consequence of which he made his evaluation or refused to say that those properties always deserved the particular evaluation he gave them, then his judgment would not be a legitimate one. (Think of someone saying "All war is wrong but I have no idea why" or "All war is wrong, but WWII was right." Could we understand these as significant moral judgments?) But the question remains: "Is $U_1$ a sufficient condition for the justification of moral claims?"

The answer to this question must be negative for several reasons. First, $U_1$ will allow as fully justified a principle held in a dogmatic, unquestioned, and insensitive way so long as it is maintained consistently. This means that if person A goes through a rigorous and imaginative exploration to see if he can consistently hold principle y and B maintains not-y in a consistent but totally unexplored and dogmatic way, then we have to conclude that A and B have equally justified claims. This conclusion offends what is usually meant by 'justified.' As was said before, consistency which is not based on some kind or rational inquiry is mere dogmatism and not a criterion for any kind of justification.

Second, $U_1$ cannot give an adequate account of justification because it has no interpretation of the concept of 'objectivity' or 'correctness' in morals. That is, many people believe that there is an objectively right or wrong way to act in moral situations, even though they might not know what it is. Although criteria for the uses of 'right' and 'correct' may differ depending upon which context one is in, one of the aspects of their meanings which does not change from field to field is that if x is objectively right, then not-x cannot be right. If contradictories can both be correct, then anything can be correct; and if anything can be correct, then the differentiation of correct from incorrect is insignificant and makes no sense. Yet this is exactly what we must say if we accept $U_1$ as the only rule of justification in morals, for if two persons make value judgments which are antithetical but held consistently by their respective proponents, then each judgment can claim to be correct.

Hence, what needs to be developed is a concept of a reasoning process which one must go through in order to be able to universalize his principles and which can give sense to the notion of correctness in morals. This will be exceedingly difficult to do both because it is so easy to assume an unjustified normative principle as the basis of this reasoning and because the views on what it means to be moral are so diverse that it seems no general agreement on what constitutes moral reasoning is possible. Yet such a concept must be developed if we are to understand how morals can both allow freedom of choice in values and still demand that this choice be subject to rational criticism. The next chapter will attempt to develop such a theory.

CHAPTER 6

A CONCEPT OF MORALS

6.1 Is there a concept of morals which, on the one hand,
does not assume a normative principle and thereby eliminate freedom in morals, and, on the other, gives a substantial enough account of moral reasoning not to permit as justified maxims and acts
which most people would consider morally repugnant? Is there a
concept of morals that can concomitantly do justice to such important ideas as having concern for the interests of all people, acting according to moral law and authority, having freedom of choice,
and attempting to find what is morally correct? I believe that if
morals is defined in the following way, then these questions can
be answered. Morals is that point of view whose function is to
prescribe how one ought to act and whose four main rules are: (1)
one's moral principles must be held consistently, (2) in making a
moral decision one must be cognizant of how his act will affect
its recipients' interests, (3) in making a moral decision one must
be able to imagine empathetically how each person affected by his
act will feel, and (4) one must test his moral principles thoroughly against hypothetical examples.

Morals is classified as a 'point of view' or 'stance' because
it is a way of thinking and acting rather than a definite kind of
activity like cooking, driving a car, or doing a scientific experiment. While we can be moral or act morally in almost any kind of
activity, there is no definite action which is by definition moral.
For instance, hitting a person, killing someone, taking what does
not belong to you, etc., are all acts which might be morally good,
immoral, or non-moral depending on a variety of factors, including
circumstances, effects, and what principles one holds. Because
morals is a method of making decisions and a way of acting, its
principles can be transcontextual and this is why they can apply
in almost any activity. This is not to say that morals does not
also function like a context, for, like every meaningful language,
it does have a purpose and rules. Its difference from other contexts is constituted by the universality of the scope of its rules
--they are applicable always and everywhere.

That the general function of the moral point of view is to
prescribe how one ought to act is common to all the major concep-
tions of morals. To take the moral point of view is to try to
find what one ought to do. There are, of course, secondary purposes of moral language such as giving advice, condemning, encour-
aging, imploring, etc., but these are all sub-classes of prescrib-

ing actions. While all moral judgments are prescriptions, there are many kinds of prescriptions that are not moral judgments (e.g., directions for driving to London, cooking cheese soufflé, planting corn). That which distinguishes moral prescriptions from other kinds of prescriptions is a set of rules which an agent must follow if his decision is to be a moral one. The first and most important of these rules is that one must universalize his moral claims.

The principle of universalization has been central to morals from the time that Socrates implicitly used it in his attempts to make others realize the limitations and inconsistencies of their normative views to the explicit recognition of it by both Kant and Hare as the fulcrum of moral reasoning. As stated several times before, what the principle of universalization minimally requires is (a) that one know what the properties are in virtue of which he makes his moral evaluation, and (b) that one be willing to make the same evaluation of the properties whenever they occur again, be it in a real or an imaginary case. The principle of universalization in this form $(U_1)$ is necessary to the moral point of view because in order for any value judgment to be legitimate, one must be able to give reasons as to why he evaluates the person (event, thing, act, etc.) the way he does, and once these reasons are stated, then in order to be linguistically consistent, one must make the same evaluation whenever those properties occur again. As Hare has shown, this principle is a logical one and not a normative principle, for it allows one to evaluate anything in any way. However, once the evaluation is made, it must be held consistently.

As in prudence, what the principle of universalization does in morals is make one go beyond his immediate feelings and the pressing circumstances of a situation to base his decision of what to do on more objective grounds. For instance, Joe's immediate reaction to having his wife raped is to have the apprehended rapist put to death. But then he tries to see if he can universalize the maxim "All rapists should be put to death" and imagines a case in which his son becomes very intoxicated, is to some degree lured by a not altogether innocent victim, and rapes her. He should be punished, of course, but put to death? This he cannot accept and, therefore, he cannot act on his initial maxim. The process of universalizing has forced him to be more objective in making his evaluation, for he found he could not morally do what his initial feelings demanded.

Universalization also makes illegitimate in morals any reference to singular or individualized entities such as 'I,' 'me,' 'America,' 'Yale,' 'Republicans,' 'Turks,' etc. Insofar as these kinds of words are used as names to indicate or point to certain individuals (rather than being used to stand for a certain set of properties), they cannot play a role in moral deliberation because they do not state properties or characteristics.[1]  I cannot morally say "It is right because I did it" or "It is right because the U.S. did it" where 'I' and 'the U.S.' are used as names and not to stand for descriptions. However, if I replaced 'I' with 'a person with desires x, y, z' and 'the U.S.' with 'one's homeland' then these prescriptions can become legitimate candidates for moral discussion. The difference in the two kinds of statements is significant, for while I might always favor what I do or the U.S. does, I might have grave reservations about saying that anything a person with desires x, y, z does is right, or that anything anyone's homeland does is right. The merely subjective viewpoint is eliminated; one must base his moral decisions on reasons, and reasons are inherently universal.

However, this preliminary concept of universalization as linguistic consistency ($U_1$) does nothing to distinguish morals from any other evaluative language (such as prudence), for every evaluative language requires that one have reasons for and be consistent in his value judgments. Nor does this concept help solve the problem of consistency's becoming equivalent to pig-headed obstinacy. What is it that distinguishes morals from other evaluative languages?[2]  How can the universalization rule be prevented from becoming dogmatic stubbornness?  The answer to both of these questions lies in requiring that a moral agent perform a certain kind of rational examination in order to make moral decisions and hold moral principles. If this examination is different from those of the other prescriptive languages, then it can serve to differentiate morals from them, and if one must go through a rigorous exploration before he can universalize his principles, then this would eliminate the possibility of universalization becoming equivalent to dogmatism. Hence, our major question now becomes: "What kind of examination is required in order for a person to be able to make moral decisions and to universalize moral maxims?"

6.2 One of the rules which must be followed in any moral deliberation is that the agent has to determine the facts of the case he is judging. The reason for this is obvious: if one's evaluation is not based on the facts of the situation, then it is simply not an evaluation of that situation but of some other imaginary case. If it is said that Mary ought to be punished because

---

[1] A property is minimally defined as any characteristic which is multiply-repeatable (it can logically occur at any time or place). Individuals can only be in one place at any one particular time.

[2] The answer which Hare seems to offer to this question is that morals is the most authoritative prescriptive language. That this cannot be proven has been discussed in 1.7.

she cheated on a test and she, in fact, did not cheat, then the evaluation is totally null. To make any kind of value judgment involves knowing what it is that one is judging.

However, to say that one ought to know the facts of the case is a platitude and unhelpful, because any situation will involve an infinitude of facts. Consider a case involving whether Amy ought to lie to her mother concerning her relationship with Bill. Some of the facts of the situation are the number of hairs on Amy's head, the weight of her fingernails, and color of her mother's clothes, the size, shape, color, age, and material of the room they are in, etc. It can be seen that if 'knowing the facts of the case' meant 'knowing all of the facts' we could then never make any moral judgment because we could never come to know all the facts. Thus, 'knowing the facts of the case' must, if it is to have any practical value, mean 'knowing the relevant facts of the case.' But, what are the criteria for deciding whether a fact is relevant or not? Prima facie it would seem that the relevant facts of the case are those properties or conditions in virtue of which the moral evaluation is made. For example, if I hold that in order for an act to be morally right it must produce as much happiness as possible for everyone, then the relevant facts of any situation would be those concerned with how much happiness was being created for each person.

However, if what is a relevant fact is dependent upon what values one holds, then we have reversed the order of reasoning with which we began this discussion. We started by saying that evaluations must be based on facts; now it seems that what counts as a fact is based upon what values one holds. This causes a serious problem which is evidenced by the following example. Suppose A holds that the fact that Mary and Joe are of different races is reason enough to claim that they ought not to get married, while B holds that this fact is totally irrelevant in deciding the issue. How can this dispute be adjudicated, for the disputants refuse to agree on which facts are relevant to solve the moral problem? They have chosen what facts they think are relevant according to the values they hold, and they hold different values. If one is free to choose what facts are to count as relevant, then we are back to universalizability's being equivalent to mere linguistic consistency and the problems of dogmatic stubbornness that this causes. If one is free to choose what facts are relevant, then he can simply refuse to recognize any other facts as being important and hold his opinion in a blind and unthoughtful way.

This conundrum can be solved only if we find a certain set of facts which must be taken into account in making a moral decision no matter what one's values are. I think there is one such set of facts: the effects of one's acts on the interests of its recipients. That is, in order for a person's decision to be called a moral one, he must be aware of the effects of that act on the interests of others and himself.[3] Three kinds of data can be given to support this claim. Firstly, it seems almost analytic to the concept of morals that its scope of application is the agent's interactions with others. One can have a personal 'ethic' that can guide his actions which are concerned mainly with his own welfare and development, but he cannot have a personal 'morals' in this sense. To call a man moral is not to say something about his private life, but about his relations with others. Further, morals is concerned with one's interactions with others at the highest and most important level; it transcends and can overrule any other interactional discipline such as etiquette, economics, and politics. As we discovered in the first part of this treatise, to deal with others in the most important way is to deal with their interests. Hence, if morals is a discipline concerned with one's interactions with others at the most important level of their relationships, then it is imperative to anyone attempting to make a moral decision that he be aware of the interests of those affected by his act.

Secondly, the dispute over who is to count as a patient of moral acts gives evidence for the claim that the interests of those affected by an act are always relevant facts in moral decisions. Although most people restrict the sphere of morals to interactions among persons, there are many who think one should act morally toward animals, and even some who think that all living things should be dealt with morally. Often, in attempting to make us see that we ought to extend our concept of the moral sphere to animals or other living things the advocates of these positions try to make us see that animals or other living beings have interests--they can lead better or worse lives--and thus are worthy of moral respect. What this dispute (which I will not attempt to resolve) seems to manifest is that the extent to which one is willing to view other beings as having interests is the extent to which he is willing to extend his concept of the sphere of morals.

The third kind of evidence for the thesis that the interests of others are always relevant facts in making moral decisions comes from an area which initially appears to be the strongest antagonist to this theory, deontological morals. Prima facie, deontological theories seem to contend that in order to be moral all one has to do is follow certain general moral laws or rules.

---

[3]This is not at all the same as the utilitarian position, for it does not advance that one ought to act for the greatest welfare of all; it only says that in making a moral decision one must be aware of the interests of others affected by it.

Being aware of the interests of others has nothing to do with these kinds of decisions, for all one need know is what moral laws apply to the situation in question. However, once one attempts to go beyond these first-order kinds of decisions in deontological morals, he discovers that the recognition of people's interests is crucial in determining both what makes a law a moral one and what makes an authority a moral authority.

How does one know that a principle or rule is a moral one rather than, for instance, a rule of etiquette, a family household rule, or a societal class rule? I can imagine two possible answers: either a person grasps that moral laws are those, the keeping or breaking of which has a profound effect on the interests of the people of a community (in which case one must have knowledge of the interests of people to recognize a law as moral), or, more likely, he will consider laws to be moral because he has been told that they are moral by someone he recognizes as a moral authority. But how does one recognize certain authorities as moral ones? Why, for instance, do many people recognize the church as a moral authority? I suppose people believe the church to be a moral authority because they believe it represents the word of God. But why do they think it represents the word of God? Here there are probably many reasons, but one of them must be that people recognize the church as representing God's laws because they recognize that these laws have something significant to do with human interests.

To make this point clearer, imagine the following case. We meet a wild-eyed inspired youth coming out of the mountains with a band of followers. He announces that he has spoken with God, has the power of God within him, and knows God's laws. Many sick people come to him and he heals them of serious ailments. Then he speaks and tells us that God has given him the following moral laws: "Build up piles of rocks." "Kill everyone whom you do not like." "Collect broken twigs." "Sexually subdue and conquer any person that you wish to and can." Would we recognize this person as a spokesman for God who brings us the moral law or as some deranged crackpot who somehow has acquired the power of healing some sicknesses? The latter, I am sure, would be the usual response, and this is because the laws given are either indifferent to or totally neglectful of human interests.

It appears, then, that in order to recognize any law as a moral one, deontological theories must see it as dealing with human interests or based on an authority cognizant of those interests. The reason why a person using general laws need not refer directly to the interests of others in making his moral decisions is that he already believes (perhaps sub-consciously) that the author of the law has taken into account (better than the person ever could) the interests of all human beings. From this and from the previous two arguments it can be concluded that the second major rule (universalization is the first) that must be followed in making moral decisions is that a person be cognizant of the effects of his acts on the interests of the patients of those acts.

Although this rule may appear extremely difficult to follow, it should be remembered that the important recipients of most acts are the family or close friends of the agent. The great majority of us are not in positions where we can drastically affect the lives of many people; the effects of our acts often fall on the same few persons. This being so, it is obvious that one of the best ways to determine what is in another's interests is simply to talk with him about what he considers to be in his interests. It may be somewhat simple-minded to say that many of our disastrous acts could have been prevented by better communication, but it is also very true. Communicating with others whom we know is an essential and not too arduous way of becoming aware of their interests, but it must be combined with a keen sensitivity and observation of behavior in that people are often mistaken about what is in their best interests. The matter is far more difficult when one's acts do affect a great number of people, for in these cases one cannot deal with individual interests and feelings but must think in terms of what human beings in general desire or need, and this often is inadequate. Perhaps, this is why the Greek philosophers were so opposed to large political institutions in which the acts of a few men had important effects on many people whom they could not know. There does seem to be a serious rift between gaining power over large numbers of people and being able to be moral in acts which affect those people.

6.3 It is one thing to know the interests of others, but quite another to decide how to act in light of this knowledge. When one acts morally should he do what is in the best interests of all? of his friends? of himself? or, perhaps, not worry about these interests whatsoever? To make a claim for any of the above answers, or any answers like them, would involve making a normative principle definitive of the moral point of view. This we have found to be an illegitimate thing to do because it collapses the distinction between 'good morals' and 'morals' and disallows any moral argumentation. However, we can say on purely logical grounds that one must treat the interests of every person equally unless there is some good reason for differentiating between them. This rule must be followed because the principle of universalization demands it: if one is going to act differently towards two people, then there must be some reason to differentiate them. If they both have the same properties, then one can not legitimately treat them differently.[4]

---

[4] That the principle of universalization demands that we treat all people equally unless there is a reason for differentiating them is taken from Hare's Freedom and Reason 7.3.

This does not help us very much, though, because we do not yet know what counts as a 'good reason' for differential treatment in morals. The universalization principle applies to all evaluative discourses--what partially distinguishes them are the kinds of reasons each will allow for acting differently towards different people. We found that in prudence one could justify treating people differently if there was a difference in the outcome on his own interests. What kinds of reasons is it permissible to give in the moral point of view for treating different people differently?

A possible answer to this question is that what will count as a reason for differential treatment of people will depend upon one's moral values. If one's moral principles include that Americans should be favored over all other peoples and that the interests of one's family should be advanced over those of other families, then he will treat non-Americans and non-family members differently from Americans and the members of his family. But can any value be a morally legitimate reason for treating different people differently? Is one free to act in any discriminatory way he wishes? Again, we cannot differentiate between good and bad discriminatory reasons by assuming a normative principle, because this would be making a particular value an essential part of our concept of morals, and this cannot be justified. Rather than using a normative principle for distinguishing between legitimate and illegitimate reasons for differential treatment, morals demands that one go through a process of empathetically imagining how each of the recipients of his act will feel before he can claim that his reason for differential treatment is moral. To imagine empathetically what the patients of one's acts will feel means that one both understand what those feelings will be and have at least a partial correspondence of his feelings with those of the patients. If pain is to be felt by one of the patients, then the agent should attempt to remember as vividly as he can the kind of pain that he thinks the person will feel. If a judge is trying to decide morally whether to send a convicted criminal to jail he must not only attempt to imagine as best he can the pain, misery, and depression of the criminal if he sends him to prison, but also the insecurity that would be felt by many members of the community if he were not jailed and the pain that would be suffered by some members of the community if that person, while free, committed more crimes. Notice that the rule that one must attempt to experience empathetically what the patients of one's acts will feel does not demand that the judge (or anyone) act one way rather than another; all it requires is that one must go through this process in order to make a moral decision.

A comparison of this rule (hereafter to be designated as rule 3) with the rule that one should be aware of how his act will affect the interests of others (rule 2) might be instructive in manifesting what rule 3 brings to the concept of morals. It

81

may appear that rule 3 is just a sub-class of 2, for if a person must be aware of how his acts affect the interests of everyone, then he must also be aware of how those affected will feel. The key difference between the two is contained in the difference between the phrase 'know' or 'be cognitively aware of' and 'empathetically imagine.' Look at the following example. Suppose that in the future our cognitive methods become so powerful and refined that we are able to determine the interests of everyone and put these data into a computer to which everyone has access. The computer can also accurately predict the effects of anyone's acts on those interests. Ed, who is married to a very loving wife and who is the father of a young child, meets Joan and they become wildly desirous of each other. He now tries to decide whether he can morally justify having an affair with Joan, and, following rule 2, asks the computer what the effects will be on the interests of all involved. He gets the following information: Ed: interest +8; Joan: interest -2; wife: interest -20; child: interest -35. Ed looks at these data, says "Very interesting," and goes ahead with the affair. He thinks of others and their interests in the same sense that he thinks about chemicals and their atomic numbers. His reaction to learning the effects of his acts on the interests of others is similar to his reactions on seeing a certain physics experiment for the first time. In short, Ed thinks about and treats other human beings as things or entities. To learn of their interests and feelings is to learn mere data that might as well be about rocks or integers.

What rule 3 demands above and beyond rule 2 is that if a person's thinking is to be moral, then he must think about human beings humanly. The moral stance is one which does not approach human beings as mere data or objects, but which inherently attempts to understand them in their essence of being alive, feeling beings. The moral point of view is that stance in which we treat all human beings as human beings, or as Kant would say, as ends in themselves rather than as means only. But what does it mean to treat other humans as humans or as ends in themselves? It can't mean acting always to enhance the interests of all, for this is impossible in that many acts by their very nature enhance the interests of some and lessen those of others (think of a judge's decisions). What I think it means to treat others as ends is that one consider their feelings and interests as though they were his own feelings and interests. This can only be done by empathetically imagining how other people would feel. I think that this also captures the meaning of the Golden Rule, which can not literally mean "Do unto others as you would have them do unto you" but rather "Consider the interests and feelings of others as you would have them consider your interests and feelings." Thus, one justification for why rule 3 is essential to moral reasoning is that it captures what many people feel to be the essence of what it means to be moral: treating other human beings as ends in themselves, as human beings.

Another justification for rule 3 is that it expresses the concept of impartiality, and if any one notion is analytic to the concept of morals, it is the concept of impartiality. If we find that someone has been partial or biased in his decisions, then we automatically declare that he has not been moral. To say "This judgment has been made in a biased and partial way and is a moral decision" seems to be self-contradictory. But what does it mean to be morally impartial? It cannot mean that we treat everyone in the same way, for this is an utter impossibility. Nor can it mean that we attempt to advance everyone's interests equally, irrespective of who they are or what they have done. I am far more concerned with my family's welfare than the welfare of those I barely know; yet, I do not consider this to make me immorally partial. What must be meant by moral impartiality is not equal treatment but equal consideration of interests and feelings. To be impartial means that in making decisions about what to do one considers equally the interests and feelings of all those who would be affected by his act. Considering interests and feelings is not the same as knowing them, for one could know that Mary desires to have a raise in salary, but not feel or respond to its urge or demand. To 'consider' someone's interests and feelings goes far beyond knowing what they are as facts; it involves treating those interests and feelings as though they were one's own; and this can only be done in an experience in which one attempts to imagine what it would be like to have the interests and feelings of the other person. Again, notice that being impartial does not mean that one cannot act to the detriment of some and the enhancement of others; it only means that in deciding how he is going to act one must give equal and empathetic consideration to the interests of all who might be affected by his act.

Thus, the rule that one must empathetically imagine how the recipients of his intended act will feel is an expression both of the humanness and the impartiality of the moral viewpoint. This may appear to be an odd combination, for impartiality is often associated with "being cold and unfeeling"--the impartial judge is depicted as totally unmoved by feeling or sentiment. What I have tried to show is that the truly impartial person is fully moved by feelings--the feelings of all those involved as patients of his decision. Because he is responding to a much wider scope of interests than most people ordinarily do, the impartial person can appear to be cold and unfeeling, especially to someone who expects him to respond to the usual partial feelings which blindly favor some people's interests over those of others. Being impartial and being sensitive to the wants, needs, and feelings of people are far from antithetical concepts; they are mutually interdependent and both necessary if one is to take the moral point of view.

We began this discussion with the question of what kinds of reasons were legitimate in morals for treating different people differently. The answer is that any reason is legitimate so long as it is the product of an investigation which has attempted to imagine empathetically what each of the recipients of an intended act will feel. If treatment of people is to be unequal it must at least be based on an equal consideration of everyone's feelings and interests. However, this rule also applies in those cases in which everyone is treated equally. Even though we rarely think of equal treatment as being immoral or non-moral, there are some cases in which equal treatment of everyone can overlook important differences that should be taken into account (Should one divide food equally between the starving and the well-fed?) and other cases in which an agent treats all people equally--like dogs. These kinds of cases also demand a sensitive awareness to the feelings of those involved, if the decision is to be moral. One cannot treat everyone like dogs or ignore significant differences between people and do it morally without empathetically imagining how the recipients of his act will feel, for one cannot take the moral point of view in any case unless he is willing to think impartially and humanely, and this involves the sympathetic consideration of the feelings of all the patients of one's acts.

6.4 These two rules--that one must attempt to know the effects of his act on its recipients' interests and that he must attempt to imagine empathetically how persons will feel as patients of his act--have been discussed in the context of making a decision in a specific situation involving specific identifiable people. However, even though the agent may be worried only about what to do in this one situation, he, nonetheless, must act on a principle which is inherently universal. That is, if an agent says "I ought to do x here and now because that would be in my family's best interests," then he holds the principle that it is right for one to enhance his family's interests. Because principles are, by definition, universal, they apply not only to the agent's specific case, but to many other possible cases, too. Thus, in order to be able to hold his principle in a consistent way, an agent must be willing to say it is right not only in a specific case he is facing, but in any case in which it might apply. It might be easy to hold the principle "Enhancing the interests of one's family is right" in a situation in which one's family's interests can be advanced without anybody else's suffering very much, but it is much more difficult to call the act of one's neighbor right when he advances the interests of his family to the great detriment of one's own.

This requirement that one must assent to his principle in all cases in which it applies is nothing more than has already been discussed as what one must do in order to universalize ($U_1$) his moral maxims. This procedure usually involves using one of the oldest and most effective techniques of conceptual thought: testing one's principle against hypothetical examples. Socrates used this method many times, as in the instance when Polemarchus tried to advance the principle that one should do good to his friends and harm to his enemies. Socrates asked him to consider the case in which his friends happened to be bad men and his enemies good. Is it right to do good to the bad and bad to the good? Polemarchus quickly withdrew his principle. Even though this technique is a common one, two problems must be solved in order for it to be unambiguous and effective in morals: (1) What processes must one go through in order to say that he has 'tested' his principle in a hypothetical case? (2) To what extent is an agent required to test his principles against possible cases in order to say that he can accept it as a universal principle?

The first problem has to do with a case such as A's saying "Sure, I could call my neighbor's act right even if it was to my family's detriment," but making no effort to imagine vividly what it would be like to experience such a situation. Does one only have to be able to say "I can assent to my principle in this situation," or are there certain processes one must complete in order to be able to make this kind of assertion? What constitutes "testing one's principle against a hypothetical example?" If it is necessary to follow rules 2 and 3 in order to make a moral decision about an actual case, then it is also necessary to follow them in considering hypothetical examples, because what it means 'to consider a hypothetical case' is to treat it as though it were an actual case. One finds that it is easier to follow rule 2 in hypothetical cases than in actual ones because the interests of the people involved are hypothetically constructed rather than being the object of a difficult empirical search. However, one still has to be able to predict realistically what kind of effects his act would have on people if they did have those kinds of interests. Once this is done, then the agent must apply rule 3 and attempt to imagine empathetically how those hypothetical people would feel as patients of his act. This is the key rule in testing hypothetical cases for it requires one to think and consider these people as if they were real and had real wants, desires, and interests.

To exemplify this process of testing a principle, suppose A is attempting to see if he can universalize the maxim "No one should be allowed to drink liquor." Since he and all his friends hate alcohol, he has very little problem applying this principle in his immediate surroundings. But then he attempts to imagine a case in which the people involved get a tremendous degree of satisfaction from drinking liquor, never overdrink, never get ill effects from it, and never endanger the interests of others by their moderate drinking. He correctly predicts that applying his principle to these people would cause them to lose a lot of pleasure, and tries to imagine how they would feel. "But I can't imagine how they would feel," says A "because I have no idea what it is like not to be able to drink liquor when you want to." We might, then, knowing him to be an avid coffee drinker, ask him how he would feel if he were not allowed to have coffee any more. He now imagines vividly how those people would feel, and since he could not assent to others causing him to have that kind of feeling, he decides he cannot assent to his principle. This is the kind of process one must go through to test his principle against a hypothetical case: he must predict what effects his act would have on the people of the example and attempt to imagine empathetically how each of them would feel to see whether he could still assent to his act if he had their feelings and interests.

The second problem with hypothetical examples is much harder to solve. To what degree is one obligated to test his principle against hypothetical cases before he can say that he can fully assent to it as a moral principle? Must he test it thoroughly? partially? not at all? in a piecemeal way as others raise objections? This decision must be between having to test one's principle thoroughly or not at all, for the inbetween realm of "some cases" or "to some extent" makes little sense, as one can always bring up innumerable favorable examples to support his principle. For instance, the liquor prohibitionist could test his principle against such cases as Joe's killing himself in a car accident while drunk, Mary's getting cirrhosis of the liver from drinking, Ed's beating his kids while drunk, and so on. This is really no kind of test for one's principle at all, for it does not attempt to deal with cases that might cause one great difficulty.

Before being able to decide whether moral principles must be tested thoroughly or not at all, we should be clear on what it means to test a principle thoroughly. It cannot mean testing it against all possible cases in which it might apply, for these will be infinite in number. It must, therefore, mean that one should attempt to test his principle against the hardest possible cases for it. If one can still hold his principle in these cases, then he can obviously assent to it in all other less difficult cases. But what is the hardest possible case for a principle? What are the rules for a construction of hypothetical cases that are legitimate tests for a moral principle?

The first rule for constructing hypothetical cases is obvious: the example must be relevant to the principle. What makes any example relevant to a moral maxim is that it contains those properties in virtue of which the moral evaluation is being made. To test the claims "One ought to advance the interests of his family," "Mary is good because she is nice to people," and "One ought to seek happiness," an agent needs to use examples which deal respectively with someone's advancing the interests of his family, someone's being nice to people, and someone's seeking happiness.

The second rule for constructing those hypothetical cases which are the most difficult for one's principle is that the specific circumstances of the example should be such as to challenge or conflict with one or more of the agent's basic interests or values. Moral principles usually express one value or interest of a person, but conflict in certain instances with other of his values or interests. When this conflict occurs, then the principle receives a severe test in which it can be assented to, rejected, or modified in light of the example. The best way to understand how this rule works is to look at several examples.

Suppose A strongly believes in truth-telling and wants to see if he can hold the principle "It is never right to lie." In order to test this he constructs an example in which someone lies and by so doing brings about far more happiness than would otherwise have been effected (e.g., the Jewish mother lying to the Gestapo agent concerning the whereabouts of her son). Since A also strongly values happiness, he now has a difficult time accepting the principle never to lie. He cannot just throw it out as a value, and so modifies his principle to say "Never lie unless by so doing you create substantially more happiness than otherwise could be effected." This is a much more cumbersome principle than "Never lie" but it better expresses A's values.

Suppose that B holds the principle "Create the greatest amount of happiness for the greatest number of people." He wants to test this principle and so imagines an example in which the only way for the greatest happiness to be achieved is by his sacrificing his life (e.g., a grenade comes in a room and the ten other men can be saved only if B jumps on the grenade rather than out the window). As B greatly values his survival he is no longer so sure that he wants to hold his principle in its absolute form. He might decide to modify his principle by adding the clause "except in cases in which the agent will lose his own life in order to create happiness." If he does decide to hold the principle in its simple unchanged form, he will at least be far more aware of what that principle means and what it would demand of him.

It can be seen that in order to follow this rule for the construction of hypothetical examples one needs, first, to know what his chief values and interests are and, second, to be honest with himself in setting up the most difficult conflict he can and resolving it in the way he would if he were actually faced with the conflict. If a person has values which conflict with the principle being tested and which are more important than the ones against which he actually attempts to test it, then, he has

87

not tested his principle thoroughly. If he says to himself "I could accept the negative consequences of this principle" when in fact he couldn't if the example really happened, then he is lying to himself and has not tested his principle thoroughly. To test a principle thoroughly requires that one put one's most important values, which might conflict with the principle, against that principle and then attempt to imagine vividly what it would be like to experience that case.

This may be what it means to test one's principles thoroughly but the question remains: must one do this in order to hold his principle in a moral way? As has been said, the choice is between thoroughly testing a principle and not testing it at all, for any kind of inbetween position of haphazard or piecemeal testing is really no testing whatsoever. But not testing a principle whatsoever means that one holds it dogmatically and without grounds. Are dogmatism and morals compatible? Imagine A saying that one of his moral principles is to harass anyone who does not go to church. We ask him to consider cripples who might not be able to go. Could he assent to being harassed if he got terribly sick and couldn't go? What if he changed religious beliefs--could he then assent to being harassed for the rest of his life? To all of these questions A says "There is no need for me to consider any of these cases; all I know is that I follow this principle consistently in my life. I have never tried to test this principle, nor do I know of anyone else who has; yet I believe in it fully." Would we want to grant this belief the designation of being a 'moral principle'? If we do, then there can be little reason as to why moral beliefs should be considered important and held in the esteem that they are, for they now can represent merely the dogmatic whims of a thoughtless man. Why seek moral advice? Why praise a man for being moral, for anyone who is pig-headed enough can be moral? If morals is to be considered the discipline by which men ought to guide their interactions with one another, if moral principles are to be significant, then there must be some procedure by which its principles can be tested.

This required procedure is the testing of one's principles in both actual and hypothetical cases. Every application of a moral principle in a specific situation constitutes a test of whether an agent can assent to his principle, for to act morally demands that one be cognizant of and sensitive to how his act affects the feelings and interests of its patients. To act on one's principles in an authoritarian way, insensitive to how one's acts affect others, is not to act in a moral way. However, one cannot test his moral principles only, or even mainly, in actual cases, both because experimenting with principles on actual people could be disastrous and because it often is logistically impossible to put oneself in the circumstances necessary for testing them. Thus, one must attempt to construct the most difficult hypothetical cases

88

for his principle, attempt to imagine them as vividly as possible, and then see if he could still assent to his principle being followed in them.

The only other method of justification which has been used extensively in moral discourse is appeal to moral authorities. Many people do not try to test their principles themselves but rely on the authority of their religion, family, government, etc., for justification. But in order to believe that another person or institution is a moral authority one must think that the authority (or whomever the authority depends upon) has tested its principles. If one thought that some institution held its principles entirely arbitrarily--without any kind of reasons for them--then he probably could not accept that institution as a moral authority. Thus, cases in which a person attempts to justify his claims by an appeal to a moral authority must ultimately involve a belief that the authority (or the authority's authority) has thoroughly tested the principle in question.

The fourth rule of moral reasoning has, therefore, been established: an agent must test his principle thoroughly against hypothetical cases and be able to assent to it in all these cases or, if he acts according to an authority, then he must have reason to believe that the authority has so tested its principles. Unless an agent does this, he cannot claim to hold a universalized principle. This is the concept of universalization ($U_2$) that we have been seeking, for it eliminates the possibility of holding a moral principle in a consistent but dogmatic way and, along with the other three rules of moral reasoning, can distinguish the moral point of view from other prescriptive standpoints. To make a moral decision means that one must know how his act will affect its recipients' interests, empathetically imagine how the patients of the act will feel, and test the principle upon which he wishes to act against the hardest cases for him to assent to it. To do this is to think morally; to act on principles derived from this kind of thinking is to act morally.

6.5 Is this concept of moral reasoning an adequate account of rationality in morals? Imagine the following case. We meet a being, who, by making totally accurate predictions and passing other tests, convinces us that he always and completely follows the rules of moral reasoning. In testing his maxims against hypothetical examples he always chooses those cases which are hardest for him, accurately predicts what effects any act he might do would have on the interests of its recipients, and completely and totally empathizes with the feelings its patients would have such that his feelings are exactly as theirs would be. In acting in actual situations he can accurately predict all the effects of his acts on the interests of the recipients and fully empathizes with how they will feel as patients of his act. That is, he knows perfectly what the interests of those involved are and considers, as empathetically and as accurately as possible, both the long-term and short-term feelings that his act would cause others to feel. He, thus, is able to imagine himself fully in the position of every recipient of his act and assents to it only after placing himself in all these positions. Also suppose that what he decides to do in a specific case is different from what we think ought to be done. Would we be more likely to say "You must be wrong" or to defer to his judgment knowing that we have not (and can not) perform the reasoning operations to the extent that he has? I must assume, if we were wise enough, that we would choose the deferential course.

If this is so, then we can develop a concept of what it means for a moral act or maxim to be objectively right in principle. A moral act or maxim will be right or correct if and only if it is that act or maxim which a being who completely and perfectly follows the rules of moral reasoning would do or hold.[5] That is, if a principle or an act is the product of the most thorough reasoning process possible in morals then it will, by definition, be correct, for there are no grounds on which it can be contested. If a person holds a principle which agrees with what a being who can reason perfectly in morals would maintain, then that person holds a correct moral principle whether or not he knows it or can prove it to be correct.

But, if we are limited to the observation of human reasoning, then we can never know whether our principles and acts do or do not agree with those held by a being who can reason perfectly in morals, for human beings can never reason perfectly. In order for a person to reason perfectly in morals, he must be able to predict all the effects of his act on the interests of its recipients, and this requires that one know fully all the principles by which human beings act and react, and that one know absolutely what the interests of others are. Yet, in Part I of this treatise we found that one could be sure of what was in his (or anyone's) interests only if he had a full metaphysical knowledge of the universe, an impossible thing for man to attain. Again, mere mortals cannot fully and vividly imagine exactly what others will feel such that they not only know what others feel, but also experience themselves exactly what those other people feel. But if the rules of moral reasoning cannot be followed completely and we cannot know what answers would be given by a being who followed them perfectly, then of what good is this theory of moral reasoning?

---

[5]The question might be raised as to how one can know whether two beings, both of whom can reason perfectly in morals, would agree on what is morally right. The answer is that we cannot know that they would agree; it is an ultimate presupposition of this theory that there would be an agreement.

Three kinds of answers can be given to this question. One, I believe that most wrong is committed not by people working from mistaken principles or having evil wills, but is caused by people being ignorant of what effects their acts will have on the interests of others and themselves. If the rules of moral reasoning that have been herein prescribed make people attempt to think a bit more about how their acts affect the interests of others and to imagine more vividly how others will feel as recipients of their acts, then much will be gained in helping to eliminate that unfortunate realm of unintentional evil.

Second, this concept of morals gives us many tools by which moral disputes can be solved. Although no one can attain fully the standards of knowledge and imagination demanded by the rules of moral reasoning, people can more or less asymptotically approach these standards. The degree to which a position is based upon these standards is the degree to which it is justified. Hence, we need not accept as valid a claim consistently held by a man who is ill-informed about the interests of others and unable to imagine how others feel. On the other hand, if we consider someone to have a deeper knowledge of the effects of acts on the interests of others and a more empathetic imagination than we do, then if we are to deviate from his judgment, we should have very good reasons for doing so. This manifests why the appeal to authority is so common in morals and why it is, to a degree, a legitimate appeal.

The third argument that can be made in favor of this concept of morals is that it is able to solve the antinomy of freedom and reason such as to avoid the dilemma of being either a relativist or dogmatic doctrine. It is not a relativist position, for it asserts that there is in principle an objectively right and wrong way to act, and that if one is to be moral, then he must use his powers of empirical investigation and empathetic imagination to their utmost in an attempt to determine what the right way to act is. However, because the criteria for knowing with certainty that one's maxims or acts are right are impossible for human beings to fulfill in practice, no man can say that he knows for sure what is morally right or wrong. Thus, no person need be accepted as the authority of moral truth; each person is free to determine for himself how he ought to act. However, although an agent is free to choose any principle he wishes, he is not free to choose the way by which he must arrive at and hold this principle, if it is to be a moral maxim. His principle must be thoroughly tested against the most difficult of hypothetical cases, and when he applies this principle in actual circumstances, he must do it in the full knowledge of its effects on the interests of others and attempt to put himself in the place of all those who will be affected by his act so that he can imagine how they will feel. These excruciatingly difficult reasoning procedures are necessary precisely because of the freedom in morals--we can never be sure we have found the right principle and so we need constantly to test the ones we use. But if reasoning would be unnecessary without freedom, freedom would likewise be mere whimsey or chance if it were not conjoined with a vigorous reasoning process. This view of moarls attempts both to give every agent the freedom to choose the way of acting which he thinks is best and to require that every moral choice of action be based on an extensive and imaginative exploration of the interests and feelings of all those affected by one's act.

# CHAPTER 7

## THE MORAL PERSON

7.1 This study has not discovered what is morally right or wrong and, thus, cannot say what virtues a person must have in order to be morally good. However, this does not mean that nothing can be said about what characteristics a moral person must have, for although we do not know what is right or wrong, we do know what processes must be gone through in order for an agent to take the moral point of view. If to perform these processes a person needs some definite abilities and character traits, then we will have a ground for positing what kind of character is needed in order for someone to take the moral stance. That is, we may not be able to say what kind of character is morally good, but we can say what abilities and dispositions are needed in order for a person to be able to determine what is morally good.

We have found that to make a moral decision about a particular case an agent needs to use two kinds of reasoning methods, each of which involves several complex processes. The crux of this procedure is the testing of one's maxim against the hardest of hypothetical cases. This cannot be done unless one knows his interests and values so well that he can pick that value which will most severely test his principle, has knowledge of how certain acts affect people with certain interests, and is able to imagine vividly how the patients of the act would feel if it were committed. Second, in order to act in a specific case, an agent needs both to be cognizant of how his act will affect its recipients' interests and to imagine empathetically how the prospective patients of his act will feel. These procedures in turn demand that one gain knowledge of what is in the interests of others, learn how various acts affect those interests, and develop an ability to imagine how others will feel. The extent to which a person can fulfill these processes is the extent to which he can participate in the moral point of view.

This means that it is far more difficult to take the moral stance than most of us who like to consider ourselves moral would prefer to admit. Much more than good motives or a warm feeling towards others is needed in order to act morally. Careful and rigorous testing of principles, a determined and extensive search to attain knowledge about human beings in general and one's close acquaintances in particular, and development of a keenly sensitive imagination are all necessary if one is to think and act morally.

To become accomplished in these difficult procedures requires extensive commitments of one's energies, resources, and time. Indeed, these reasoning processes are so demanding and exacting that they cannot be performed by just anyone. Without having certain abilities and character traits it is impossible to think in these ways. In particular, one must develop the abilities to discern facts, reason logically, and imagine how people feel; and in order to exercise these abilities, a person must develop the dispositions of being objective, impartial, sensitive, and thorough.

To make a moral decision demands that one be able to discern facts about his own interests, the interests of others, and how various acts affect those interests. As we have discovered, gaining knowledge of these kinds of facts is not simply a matter of 'looking and seeing,' for it cannot be attained unless one develops such skills as being able to abstract from particular cases the universals which make those cases valuable or not valuable to oneself and others, being able to see that the activities of any particular context represent possibilities of fulfillment or dissatisfaction for people with certain skills, traits, and desires, and being able to grasp the complex connections between an act and its effects. However, even if one nurtures these fact-finding skills, they will remain ineffective without the development of a disposition to be objective, that is, a disposition to base one's decisions on reasons and not to color the facts with his emotions and values. If one constantly attempts to determine what is a fact by what he desires to be a fact, then this will have to involve distortions of what is true. For instance, one of the greatest hindrances to gaining knowledge about the interests of others is the projection onto others of one's own desires and values. Unless one develops the trait of being objective, natural tendencies like projecting one's values onto others will distort his ideas of the facts and not allow him to find what is true.

The second ability needed in order to take the moral point of view has already been laboriously discussed: the ability to imagine empathetically what the patients of one's intended acts will feel. This is an extremely difficult skill to develop because people tend to be so involved with their own desires that, if they do stop to consider the feelings of others, these are often treated only in an abstract way. But, as hard as this ability may be to develop, it is considered by many to be the crucial trait in one's becoming a social and moral being. Unless a person can learn to take the point of view of those whom his acts affect rather than just dwelling on his own desires, he will not be able to engage successfully or morally in social interactions. This ability to imagine how the recipients of one's acts will feel is intrinsically related to the character trait of being sensitive, that is, the disposition to be aware of the wants, needs, desires, and interests both of oneself and of other

people. If one is insensitive to these desires, then he will have
no basis for imagining how others will feel; his imaginative
attempts will be mere flights of fancy. Imagination of feelings
without sensitivity can produce highly romanticized or melodramatic
pictures, but it rarely is effective in understanding how real
people with complex and subtle emotions feel.

Third, in order to take the moral stance an agent must be
adept at logical reasoning. Moral decisions are very complicated
as a person must take into account the interests and feelings of
everyone involved in his act, how his possible acts will variously
affect those interests and feelings, and whether these effects
could conflict with any of his other values. Without an ability
to organize data and see what kinds of effects are consistent and
inconsistent with the various principles one holds, an agent will
not be able to take the moral point of view fully. Developing
this ability to reason well in morals is dependent on an agent's
cultivating concomitantly a disposition to be thorough and rigorous in his thinking. Someone who does not have this trait will
accept a principle after several skirmishes into hypothetical examples and applications in specific instances. The thorough person will attempt to test a principle against all his values which
might conflict with it, resist a simple formulation when the principle demands to be conditioned by other values, and, as he matures and grows and his insights and values change, he will be constantly re-examining his principle to see if he can still accept
it.

In many ways these dispositions and abilities are combined
in what is the most important moral trait, impartiality. To be
morally impartial requires that one treat all humans the same in
at least one way: he consider equally the interests and feelings
of everyone who might be affected by his acts. To consider someone's feelings and interests demands that one not only know what
those interests and feelings are (or will be) but also imagine
those feelings in an empathetic way. Thus, being impartial requires that one have skills to discern facts about the interests
of others and oneself and to imagine empathetically how others
and oneself will feel as patients of one's acts. And, as we have
seen, these skills in turn require that one develop the dispositions of being objective, sensitive, and thorough in one's search
for the facts and his attempt to empathize with the feelings of
others. It is this trait of impartiality which forces us to negate our ordinary, insensitive, and partial way of acting in the
world and to become sensitively aware of the others involved in
our actions and our effects on them; that is, it forces us to
take the moral stance.

To develop and exercise these traits and abilities fully is,
of course, an ideal. While there is no one who completely fulfills

the ideal, there is also probably no one totally devoid of the
moral dispositions and skills. Rather there is a continuum of people, decisions, and principles which are more or less moral, with
no fine dividing line between when a person's decisions and principles are moral and when they are not. Although this will not
please people who like to divide the world into black and white
categories, it does seem to fit our experience of morals better
than saying that there is a radical and clear-cut division.
Clearly, someone who has gone through a great deal of rigorous
thought in deciding what principle to follow, is sensitive to others in the application of that principle, and who always follows
his principle even when it has negative consequences for himself
is taking the moral point of view. Likewise, someone who says
that he holds a value in a moral way, but who has never thought
about or tested it, who never applies it in a sensitive way, and
who fails to act on it in circumstances in which it might be detrimental to him is probably not holding his principle in a moral
way. Most of our moral decisions seem to fall somewhere between
these two poles. The crucial question, then, is: "Where do I
stand on the continuum?" "Are my values, thinking, and actions
closer to the ideal or closer to a non-moral point of view?"
The problem and also the great challenge of morals is that one
can always become more moral, more able to make moral decisions
that are based on knowledge, empathetic imagination and thorough
reasoning. It is a life-long endeavor that requires a fundamental commitment to developing the abilities and dispositions definitive of the moral stance. The degree to which this commitment
is made is the degree to which a person is serious about being
moral. One can have all the warm feelings for humanity possible,
but without the cultivation of the powers of reasoning and imagination, there is little reason to believe that those feelings
will ever issue into any kind of effective moral action.

7.2 The moral person has been defined according to what
abilities and traits he must have in order to make a moral decision. But many people would want to say that this is inadequate,
for what counts in morals is not how a person comes to a decision
but how he acts. If someone acts to the great detriment of other
people, then he cannot be considered moral no matter how sensitive, impartial, etc., he has been in arriving at his decision.
While this critique is illegitimate in that it assumes a normative principle as being definitive of morals, it does express
the profound and common sentiment that a moral person is one who
tries to act for the betterment of all persons. Certainly, if a
moral theory could not explain why a person who followed its
rules would tend to act for the welfare of people rather than to
their detriment, it would count severely against its being an
adequate concept of morals. Can the proposed theory of morals
and the moral person account for this important sentiment?

One reason to believe that a person taking the moral stance, as it has been delineated in this treatise, would not want to act arbitrarily against another's interest and would try to aid him as best he could is that in order to act on any other view, he would have to imagine in a vivid and sensitive way cases in which his interests were either disregarded or arbitrarily thwarted and regard these cases as good. That is, to act on a maxim which entails that one not attempt to satisfy the interests of all persons as much as possible demands that one empathetically imagine himself in the place of the recipients whose interests are negated and while in that empathetic state assent to the principle's being followed. For instance, in order to maintain the principle that no one should commit an act of homosexual love even when both parties desire it and it would not harm the interests of anyone else, one must empathetically imagine what it would be like to be such a person in such a situation and then still say that he values those drives and interests being frustrated, that he could assent to living a life of sexual frustration if he were a homosexual. How many people can empathize fully with the feelings of a homosexual, know that his acts will not be detrimental to others. and still condemn those kinds of acts because of fidelity to a certain ideal of what a proper sexual act is? To take the moral stance and not wish to aid the satisfaction of interests means that one must both empathize with a person whose interests and feelings will be either ignored or intentionally frustrated for the sake of some ideal and still want the principle to be followed. This is extremely difficult to do.

Another reason for believing that a person who takes the moral point of view will decide to act in the best interests of all is evidence from experience. A person who takes the time and effort to learn what the interests of other people are, who develops a keen sensitivity to the feelings and interests of others, who can empathize with the patients of his acts, and who thoroughly tests and thinks about his principles does not usually either ignore or arbitrarily override those interests and feelings in acting. Think of someone who acts to the detriment of others' interests or without concern for those interests. Does such a person tend to be a sensitive person? Does he tend to be able to imagine empathetically how others will feel as recipients of his acts? Does he devote large portions of his energy and time to learning about what the interests and feelings of others are? While there is no analytic necessity which requires sensitive, empathetic people concerned with learning about the interests of other persons to act so as to enhance the fulfillment of those interests, experience manifests that persons with these kinds of abilities and traits do in fact act to the benefit of all to the extent that this is possible.

If utilitarianism's central insight is that being moral in-

volves attempting to enhance the amount of human satisfaction as
much as possible, then the proposed moral theory can explain why
many people attempting to be moral also tend to be, at least partially, utilitarians. Utilitarianism is, in many ways, a natural
outcome of someone's taking the moral point of view, 'natural' in
the sense that experience has shown that human beings who develop
the moral traits and abilities also desire to act for the benefit
of the interests of all people as best they can.

7.3 If this concept of a moral person explains why utilitarianism is so common and powerful a normative theory, can it also
account for the most important concepts of deontological systems:
moral law, authority, and obligation? Whether or not one accepts
a deontological position, he must at least admit that these concepts have played important roles in the moral beliefs of a vast
number of people and that if the concepts of morals and the moral
person proposed here cannot interpret these notions, then this
must count as a serious criticism of them.

There is no difference between the proposed concept of morals and the deontological one in their general regard for the cen-
trality of rules in a person's moral life. Both hold that any
moral act must be based upon a rule or principle which he is willing to follow in all cases in which it is applicable. However,
there is a major disagreement between the positions as to how
these moral rules should be conceived. Many deontologists hold
that moral rules should be unconditional simple laws commanding
that a certain act be done or avoided (e.g., "Honor thy father
and mother." "Do not lie."), while the position developed here
allows for very complex and conditioned rules such as "Do not lie
unless by so doing you either prevent a murder or create far more
happiness than otherwise would occur." At one level this disagreement dissolves, for there can be no more than one simple unconditional rule in any consistent moral system. If a person holds
two general moral rules, then there is a possibility that they
can conflict, and to solve this conflict a hierarchy must be developed which will condition one of the rules. For example, if
one wants to maintain that men ought not to kill and ought not to
steal, and that not killing is the more important rule, then the
rule against stealing would be the conditional "Do not steal unless by so doing you prevent someone from being killed." The two
positions, then, have to agree that if a moral system has more
than one rule, then conditional rules are allowable in morals.

However, the disagreement concerning the conception of
rules can re-occur at a different level in that there are two
basic ways of treating the "simple moral laws" (e.g., "Do not
lie." "Do not kill." "Do not steal.") One way--the deontolog-
ical--maintains that simple moral laws are justified independently of any end, and that they must be absolutely obeyed in all

cases except those in which two moral laws conflict, in which event one should follow the moral law which takes precedence. The other fundamental way of treating these simple moral laws is to see them as important aids or guides for the production of some general end, as justified by that end, and as breakable in cases of extreme conflict with that end. For instance, one's basic value could be producing the most amount of satisfaction for the most people, and he could find that the general observance of such rules as "Do not break promises" and "Do not lie" is so important in producing this satisfaction that these rules should be followed in all cases except where there is substantial evidence that by following them much less satisfaction will be attained. Thus, one would follow the maxim not to lie in all situations except those in which he could predict that not lying would produce far more pain than lying would, and in these cases he would lie.[1]

Which of these is the best way to treat the "simple moral laws?" The moral position that has been developed in this treatise is neutral in regards to this issue. What it requires is that in order to justify and act on any rule in a moral way, one must test that principle thoroughly and consider empathetically the interests and feelings of all those who might be affected by it each time he acts. If one is going to hold a rule in a strict deontological way--follow it no matter how it affects interests-- then he must do this in light of knowing what those interests are and empathetically imagining how those people will feel. While I think that such reasoning procedures would tend to make an agent think of the simple moral laws as guides in satisfying interests and not as absolute commands, this does not necessarily follow from these procedures. Thus, this position, like deontology, insists that morals must be a rule-governed activity and allows for the simple moral laws to play as important a role in moral thinking as the agent sees fit. What it refuses to do is to make simple moral laws analytic to the moral point of view or to demand that they be followed regardless of their effects.

Another major precept in many deontological systems is that a moral person is one who obeys a moral authority. While this is not so for deontological morals like Kant's which attempt to justify rules on the basis of reason or intution, it is true for the deontological systems that have been historically dominant-- those of religions and governments. Reference to an authority is a very important device in morals because it can give an agent both a justification for his principles and relieve him of having

---

[1]There are variations of these positions. One of the most important is a position which maintains that once rules are justified by reference to an end, then they can never be justifiably broken, not even in situations in which following the rules would thwart the end from being realized.

to go through complex and intricate testing procedures. Because a moral authority has, by definition, far more knowledge about moral matters than any individual agent, its laws and rules ought to be accepted and followed. Although this notion of a moral authority is an anathema to those ethicists who emphasize individual autonomy and freedom, it, nonetheless, has been so influential in the morals of many societies, that any concept of morals which cannot interpret it can not be fully consonant with the ordinary experience of morals.

If the theory of a moral person that has been set forth here is accepted, then we can see why the concept of a moral authority can be such a useful and powerful tool in morals. Since following the moral procedures, and developing the moral abilities and traits are so difficult and admit to such varying degrees of fulfillment, there will be some people who will be far superior to others in them. When this is so, then that person who has developed the moral traits and abilities far beyond the average person and who is able to reason through the moral procedures much better than others should be considered a moral authority and should be followed by those people who are unable through lack of ability or disposition to reason well in morals. Authorities are needed and useful because moral reasoning is so hard; if there were no authorities and everyone had to make his own decisions about every moral matter, then the ensuing state would probably be chaos. Oft times it is far better to be guided by those wiser than oneself than to attempt to rely solely on one's own inadequate insights.

However, if an agent is going to follow the principles of another person or institution, then he must have good grounds for believing that that person or institution should be considered a moral authority. He must have some kind of procedure to test the person's or institution's knowledge of human interests, ability to imagine empathetically the feelings of others, and ability to reason. Also, because no principles can be proven to be necessarily correct, any principle from any authority must be tested constantly. How is this to be done? It would seem that a crucial part of this testing must be that when an agent acts on an authority's maxim, he be aware of the interests of those people whom his act will affect and attempt to imagine how they will feel. That is, while obeying an authority might relieve one of having to test his principle thoroughly against hypothetical cases, he still needs to know the interests of the patients of his acts and be able to imagine their feelings in applying those principles. If he does not do this, then he cannot test adequately whether the source from which he received his principles should be considered an authority. Thus, while this theory permits the practice of appealing to an authority in moral matters, it does not allow one to choose or follow that authority blindly. Appea-

ling to an authority in morals is a legitimate and often wise
thing to do but only when one has substantial grounds for believing that the authority has the abilities, procedures, and dispositions necessary to the moral point of view.

The final notion of deontological morals that must be interpreted in any adequate moral theory is that of moral obligation,
for many deontologists have held that the essence of the moral experience is feeling that one is 'bound' or 'obligated' to act in
a certain way. The moral experience is one in which an agent cannot do just what he desires to do. He feels called upon to stop
his ordinary modes of behavior and ask "What am I obligated to
do?" His activity cannot be governed by the usual subjective in-
clinations but by a moral law. The proposed theory of morals attempts to capture this notion of moral obligation by requiring
of the moral agent that he stop and consider the interests of all
those whom his act will affect and base his action not on what he
feels like doing but on a principle which he has thoroughly tested and which he can accept as governing his actions in all cases
in which it is applicable. The moral experience is that experience in which the agent becomes as aware as possible of the effects
of the acts he is considering on the interests and feelings of
others and in which he finds his actions governed by a rationally
tested principle rather than his immediate wants or desires. To
be moral is to be 'bound'--bound to stop and consider the interests and feelings of others before one acts and then to act only
on a universalized principle.

7.4 The two basic kinds of normative moral positions--
deontology and utilitarianism--reflect the two traditional but
antithetical images of a moral person. On the one hand the moral
person has been depicted as a stern unwavering man who always
acts according to principles and never just according to how he
feels. He is a man of duty, bound by what he takes to be the
moral law. His relations with others are governed by principles
and not by his personal feelings for this individual or that.
On the other hand, the moral person has been viewed as a deeply
compassionate, sensitive, caring person whose love and concern
for all people far exceeds that which is ordinarily found. His
relations to others are never just instances of a general principle, for he treats all people as unique individuals and is con-
siderate of their idiosyncratic needs and wants.

The concept of the moral person herein presented has attempted to fuse together these two traditional but seemingly antithetical images of the moral person. It conceives of the moral
person as always acting according to principles, for the moral
person knows that spur of the moment action on the basis of temporary feelings can often be disastrous and that the moral viewpoint, more than any other, demands that actions have a thought-

101

ful, rational base. However, the moral person never just follows his principles automatically, blind to the interests and feelings of those people who are affected by his acts, for every time a moral person acts according to his principles, he must be sensitive to and aware of the interests and feelings of those whom his act will affect. This demands that a moral person attempt to know, understand, and relate to the people his acts affect as individuals. It is highly doubtful that a person will attempt to gain these insights into others unless he has a significant concern and love for people. Thus, this concept of the moral person sees him as constantly testing his principles by always being profoundly sensitive to those whom his acts affect and as constantly tempering his feelings and concerns for individuals by demanding that he act only on thoroughly-tested universal principles. He neither gets lost in the abstractness of universals nor overwhelmed by the intensity of immediate feelings and considerations. He is both a person of principle and a person keenly sensitive to the persons in his life whom he affects the most.

Glimpses of the life of a person attempting to be moral might involve seeing him keenly and sensitively interacting with his friends so as to better discern what their interests are, avidly reading and researching material concerning human behavior and growth, or reflecting on how he should act if he were placed in a difficult moral situation. One would find that as he matured he would increasingly demand that every act he makes be thoughtful, be done in an awareness of its effects on others. We would also find him seeking advice from, and being respectful of, those whom he considers to exemplify the moral traits and abilities to a high degree. Finally, we would discover that the moral stance is for him not one among many that he could take, rather it is the most pervasive and constant viewpoint of his life, or social life. He never lets the rules of these contexts override moral considerations. It may not be required by his business that he be sensitive to the interests of those with whom he works--it might even be bad for the business for him to do so--but he will, nonetheless, try to interact with his associates in a moral way. His family might want him always to be biased towards fulfilling its interests, yet he will consider in an impartial way the interests of all involved in his acts. No matter how the context demands that he treat other people, he always tries to treat them in a moral way.

As can be seen, being a moral person is not a state which one either attains or does not attain; rather becoming such a person is a task, an on-going endeavor in which one can always improve but which he can never complete. To become a moral person is to strive to perfect one's abilities to imagine empathetically the feelings of others and to test his principles in a rational way. It is to enter a never-ceasing quest for knowledge about people's interests and how various acts he might commit will affect those interests. It is constantly attempting to strengthen the traits of being sensitive to the needs and emotions of people, objective in the search for facts, thorough in one's reasoning, and impartial in one's considerations of the interests of those whom his acts will affect. Developing these traits and abilities and gaining the knowledge necessary to the moral point of view cannot be done only when one is faced with making a moral decision. They demand that one commit substantial amounts of time and energies to them over the course of his life. Indeed, for the person seriously concerned with becoming moral, the tasks of the moral life are not something to be accomplished in one's spare time; rather they constitute the proper vocation for human beings.

PART III: ETHICS

CHAPTER 8

PRUDENCE, MORALS, AND ETHICS

8.1 We began our investigation into ethics by raising the question, "How ought I to live?" and have since explored the two most important ways in which it can be answered: "One ought always to seek that which is in his own interests" and "One ought always to act morally." But what should a person do if he finds that what is morally demanded of him is not in his best interests? Should he live prudentially or should he live morally? This is the crucial question of practical philosophy, for all of one's actions will be affected by how he decides which of these prescriptive languages will be his highest.

The problem needs a further clarification beyond the one it received in the first chapter of this book, due to the normatively neutral way in which morals has since been defined. Since it is logically possible for a person to hold any normative principle in a moral way, someone could both be moral and maintain the prudential principle that everyone should act so as to maximize his own satisfactions. In order to hold the prudential principle in a moral way rather than merely prudentially, a person must be willing to universalize ($U_2$) it, be cognizant of the interests of those whom his acts affect, and empathetically imagine how the patients of his acts will feel. That is to say, if a person claims that it is morally right to be prudential, then he must be willing to call right any prudential act done by another agent even if it is to his great detriment, and in cases in which his interests conflict with those of other people, he must know what the interests of those people are and be able to imagine empathetically how they feel when their interests are overruled by his acts. While I think it is highly unlikely that any rational and sympathetically imaginative individual could go through these procedures and still hold the prudential principle, it is at least logically possible.

Thus, the conflict between prudence and morals cannot be expressed as that of opposed normative principles, but rather as that of opposed stances or points of view from which to act. Ought one simply presuppose that it is always right to seek what is in his interests and act in a way which does not require him

to be cognizant of interests and feelings of the people affected
by his acts, or ought one take that point of view which demands
of him that he rigorously test all his normative principles, learn
about interests of all those persons who might be affected by his
acts, and empathetically imagine how the patients of his acts will
feel?

How should one solve this problem is a conundrum, for, as
we have already discovered, there is no higher prescriptive language by which to decide whether morals or prudence is the better
point of view to take. There is no ethical 'ought' above the prudential and moral 'oughts' by which one could justify that one of
these points of view 'ought' to be chosen over the other. However, although no claim for why one ought to be moral rather than
prudential (or vice versa) can be justified, I believe it can be
shown that a person who develops the traits and abilities necessary to determine for himself what is in his best interests must
develop into a person who takes the moral point of view. This is
not to say that the best prudential policy is to be moral (for
this is probably false), but that the kind of character and abilities which are needed in order to be prudential demand of one
that he take the moral point of view, even when it is to the agents detriment to do so. The major presupposition of the argument which follows will be that although abilities and character
traits may be developed in response to only one problem or context, once these are engendered in a person they will generally
determine all of his behavior. One's experiences, emotions, and
thoughts may change quite frequently, but one's character and general abilities, while capable of slow change over a period of
time, remain relatively stable and represent more than any other
factor the enduring and pervasive aspects of a personality. They
cannot be turned on and off; where a person is, there also are
his character traits and general abilities.

8.2  As must have been already noticed, the abilities and
dispositions needed by a person to be prudential are, in general,
the same as those needed to take the moral point of view. Both
the prudential and moral person must develop the abilities to
discern facts, imagine how people feel, and reason logically.
Both must also cultivate the traits of being objective, sensitive,
impartial, and thorough. This correspondence of abilities and
dispositions indicates that there is a very close tie between a
person able to be prudential and one able to be moral. However,
there are crucial differences of description and scope of application between some of the abilities and traits as they function
in prudence and as they function in the moral point of view, and
it is these differences which represent the fundamental distinction between prudence and morals.  What I will attempt to do is
to indicate what these differences are and demonstrate why the

105

moral formulation of the differing traits and abilities is a necessary development from the prudential formulation of them.

Both the abilities of logical reasoning and imagination vary in their moral and prudential forms. The difference in the kinds of logical reasoning demanded by morals and prudence is one of scope of application, for in morals every normative claim must be rationally tested to see if it can be consistently universalized, while in prudence there is one principle which does not need to be so tested: the maxim that one ought to seek that which is in his own best interests. The kinds of imagination respectively required by these two points of view show a more radical divergence. In morals, one must develop an empathetic imagination, one which not only can grasp what another person feels but also can feel at least partially what that other person feels. However, the imagination of other people's feelings required by prudence is only abstract or predictive. That is, while one needs to know or predict how others feel in order to understand the consequences of his acts, this knowledge need not be empathetic. It may be important for A to be able to imagine that B will feel pain if he does act x, but it is not prudentially necessary to imagine that pain painfully.

There is also a difference of scope between the moral and prudential traits of sensitivity. We discovered that sensitivity was needed in prudence because one had to be aware of the needs and desires of himself and others if he was going to be successful in predicting whether an act would be in his best interests. Since a prudential person is sensitive only because it is in his interests to be so, there would be no need to be sensitive to another person if the agent thought that his feelings would have little or no bearing on the agent's interests. Morals, on the other hand, categorically demands that one be sensitive to all the possible patients of his acts, no matter how their feelings affect his interests.

Finally, and most importantly, there is a critical disparity between being prudentially impartial and being morally impartial. Although both prudence and morals require one to be impartial in the sense of treating all people equally unless there is a good reason for differentiating between them, they differ radically on what processes one must go through in order to give a good reason. In prudence all one must do is show that such differential treatment is in his best interests, while in morals no reason for differential treatment can be accepted unless one has given prior and equal consideration to the interests and feelings of all those persons who are prospective patients of his act, where 'giving consideration' involves both knowing what a person's interests are and being able to imagine empathetically how he

106

will feel as a recipient of one's act. No such process of consideration is necessary to be impartial in prudence.

It must now be shown why the moral forms of these differing traits and abilities are a natural and necessary development from their prudential forms. The keys to understanding this development are the other traits required by both prudence and morals, objectivity and thoroughness, for it is these traits which demand of one that he not stop at an incomplete or arbitrary ground for his actions, but find the most complete and justified reasons for them.

The prudential form of logical reasoning which demands that one test all his principles except the prudential maxim must, if the prudential person is thorough and objective, develop into the moral form which requires that all normative principles be tested. Thoroughness will drive the prudential person to ask the question "Why should the principle that one ought to seek that which is in his best interests be followed?" and objectivity will demand of him that he answer it not by reference to how he feels but by giving reasons. However, to demand a justification for holding the prudential principle means that one can not remain in the prudential point of view or any point of view which simply assumes a normative principle. The only way one could give reasons for the prudential principle is by taking that point of view which tests all principles and assumes none. This is precisely the moral point of view and the moral form of logical reasoning.

Likewise, thoroughness and objectivity demand that the limited sensitivity of the prudential person become the full sensitivity of morals. Insofar as a person attempts to develop any trait fully, it will begin to characterize all his actions and interactions, not just some. If one attempts to become more and more sensitive (as he must do in order to be prudential), then he will be sensitive to all those with whom he interacts and not just those whose feelings have a significant bearing on his welfare. Thoroughness will require that one ask himself "Is the fact that A's feelings will not vitally affect my interests a good reason not to be sensitive to A?" and objectivity will demand a reason for giving a positive answer to this question. However, to give such a reason will require attempting to universalize the principle that an agent can be insensitive to a person if that person's feelings will not have an important bearing on the agent's interests. But to universalize this involves one's seeing whether he could accept this principle were he in that person's place, and one can not make such a decision unless he is sensitive to the feelings, needs, and wants of that person. Thus, insofar as one must test whether or not he should be insensitive to another person, this already presupposes that he be sensitive to the person. The more a prudential person develops the traits of objectivity, thoroughness, and sensitivity, the more this trait of sensitivity must characterize all of one's interactions with people, and this is the moral form of sensitivity.

The two arguments for why prudential imagination must become empathetic are based upon the difference of the two major roles imagination plays in prudential thinking. On the one hand, a prudential agent needs to imagine how other people will feel if he is going to be able to predict the consequences of his acts on his interests. This kind of imagination need be only abstract rather than empathetic. On the other hand, the prudential person needs to be able to imagine how he will feel in the future if he makes certain decisions and this kind of imagination must be empathethic. What will I be feeling five years from now if I accept this job, or if I marry Amy, or if I decide to have a child? In answering these questions one needs to be able to do more than just predict what he will be feeling--"comfortable but a little bored," "basically content but somewhat sexually frustrated," "proud but anxious over limitations of travel and money"--he must also evaluate whether those emotional states are more worth having than other possible feelings. It is very difficult to evaluate complex emotions like these without attempting to imagine vividly how they would feel, without attempting to "try them on" before deciding whether or not to choose them. It is very easy to say that feeling comfortable but a little bored is all right if one does not attempt to imagine vividly what such a feeling over a long period would be like; it is much harder to value this state positively when one attempts to imagine empathetically what such a person (his future self) would feel. Since in order to make prudential decisions one must evaluate the kinds of feelings he imagines he will have in the future, he needs to develop an empathetic imagination.

In understanding the second argument for why prudential imagination must become fully empathetic we must first see why the prudential concept of impartiality must develop into the moral one. If the prudential person is thorough and objective, then he will have to raise the question "Why ought I imagine empathetically how I will feel as a recipient of my acts but imagine only abstractly how others will feel?" That is, he must ask "What justifies treating myself and others differently?" This is the fundamental question which differentiates the moral point of view from the prudential. This question cannot be raised within the realm of prudence because it is the ultimate presupposition of that discipline that such differential treatment ought to occur. However, if the prudential person is thorough and objective, then he must question all of his presuppositions and attempt to find reasons for them.

Once one seeks a reason for treating himself differently from other people, then he can no longer remain within prudence and must find another discipline by which to answer this question.

But the only other discipline whose prescriptive authority is not less than that of prudence is morals, and, therefore, this is the only discipline from which a reason could be given that would not be begging the question. That is to say, if one chose a lesser discipline like economics and said that one ought to treat himself differently from others because it is economically wise to do so, then the question must be asked as to why the principles of economics should be followed, and if one tries to say that it is prudential to do so, then this is begging the original question. Now, if one attempts to go through the processes of morals to determine if he ought to treat himself differently from other persons, then he also must attempt to imagine empathetically how those other persons feel because this is a necessary part of the moral procedures. Thus, the traits of being thorough and objective have demanded that the prudential person go beyond his limited concepts of impartiality and abstract imagination to develop an ability to imagine empathetically how all persons whom his acts affect will feel. They will not let him simply accept that a difference to his interests constitutes a legitimate ground for differential treatment of others, for differential treatment can only be justified after one has gone through the process of giving equal consideration to the interests and feelings of all.

What I have tried to show with these arguments is that the prudential traits and abilities are interrelated and that the effects of these interrelations require that the prudential forms of the traits and abilities develop into their moral forms. In its assumption of the normative principle that one always ought to seek what is in his best interest and in its differentiation of oneself from all other people without specifying on what grounds the differentiation is based, the prudential stance is arbitrary. Yet the prudential traits of thoroughness and objectivity will not allow one to take an arbitrary position, and thus the prudential person is forced by his very nature to take a point of view that does not assume any normative principle to be right or allow any arbitrary differentiation of people, and this is the moral point of view. Thus, if being prudential demands that one not be arbitrary in his values and reasons, then it demands of one that he hold the moral point of view to be his highest prescriptive language.

8.3  By examining the logic of the traits and abilities needed to be prudential, the above arguments have tried to demonstrate in a rigorous way that if a person develops these traits and abilities fully, then they will necessarily lead him to take the moral point of view. This conclusion is supported by what happens in our ordinary experience, for this experience often manifests that the people most able to determine what is in their best interests are the people most likely to be moral, and that moral people tend to have highly developed abilities to find

109

what is good for themselves. The key to understanding why this is so is to see that a person cannot know what the interests of others are or imagine how they will feel unless he has knowledge of himself and can imagine how he will feel, and that once a person becomes sensitive to his own interests and feelings, he must become sensitive to those of others.

To perform the moral task of grasping what is in another person's interest an agent minimally needs to understand the concept of 'a person's interest.' This is not easy, for it involves understanding a great deal about the conflicts and relations of desires, what desires tend to be more fundamental, what kinds of satisfactions tend to be lasting and which temporary, the relationships between desires, abilities, ideals, etc. It is hard to imagine that anyone can become aware of these kinds of complexities in others unless he has attempted the prudential task of being sensitive to them in himself, for one is almost never in a position to experience these kinds of intricate structures in another person. Likewise, if the agent is to be able to accomplish the moral process of empathetically imagining how another person will feel, then he must have the prudential virtues of self-knowledge of his own emotions and an ability to imagine how he would feel if certain acts were done to him. These points manifest why the most famous of Delphic inscriptions, "Know Thyself," is at the core of Greek ethics. The Greeks knew that without self-knowledge one could not find what is good--either for himself or others. Because Oedipus does not know who he is, he brings disaster to both himself and the people of Thebes.

Not only is it true that an agent cannot adequately know and imagine the interests and feelings of others without self-knowledge and an ability to imagine how he himself will feel, but it is also true that once an agent has sensitively explored himself, he will then be more sensitive to others. Developing a trait means to develop like reactions to like circumstances; if one cultivates a sensitivity to his own interests, then he will also become sensitive to the interests of beings like him. This is perhaps best seen in cases in which a person attains self-knowledge about an aspect of himself and then becomes sensitive to others like him in this respect and insensitive to others who do not have that aspect in their lives. For instance, businessmen can often be sensitive to the problems of other businessmen but unable to relate sensitively to non-business types of people, and counter-culture types of people, while often sensitive to persons like themselves, tend to be insensitive to the problems, interests, and feelings of people attempting to follow typical societal patterns. The difference between these kinds of people and the prudential agent is that the latter is sensitive to himself in the deepest and most fundamental of ways--as a whole person--and he can therefore be sensitive to others as whole persons.

This connection between being prudential and being moral is, perhaps, best expressed in the saying that how one treats others manifests how he treats himself, and how he treats himself is manifest in his treatment of others. If a person attempts to be sensitive, knowledgeable, and imaginative about his own most basic wants and needs, what gives him his deepest satisfactions, and what causes him the most frustrations and pain, then he will tend to be sensitive, knowledgeable, and imaginative to these factors in others. Likewise, indications that a person is not able to determine what is in his best interests are insensitive and thoughtless acts which cause others unnecessary suffering. Aristotle expressed this connection between a person's relation to himself and to others when he said: "Friendly relations with one's neighbors, and the marks by which friendships are defined, seem to have proceeded from a man's relations to himself . . . The bad man does not seem to be amicably disposed even to himself, because there is nothing in him to love; so that if to be thus is the height of wretchedness, we should strain every nerve to avoid wickedness and should endeavour to be good; for so and only so can one be either friendly to oneself or a friend to another."[1]

If an immoral act[2] is thought of as that which causes unnecessary human suffering, then there is further evidence for the claim that the prudential person will also be a moral person. What is the cause of most unnecessary suffering? A malicious will? Acting from wrong principles? Neither of these answers seems correct as wills dedicated to causing unmitigated pain and people consciously acting according to well-formulated but wrong principles are so rare that they could account for only a small portion of suffering. Rather the major causes of unnecessary suffering seem more clearly to be insensitivity, ignorance, and failures of imagination. The average person, while meaning well, often harms others and himself because he fails to be sensitive to some need, fails to learn what consequences his act might have, or does not

---

[1] Nichomachean Ethics, 116a, 1-3; 116b, 25-29.

[2] Because the definition of 'being moral' given in this book does not include a normative claim, it cannot have as its opposite 'being immoral' or 'being evil' but only 'being non-moral.' However, I think that in most normative moral positions unnecessary human suffering is seen as evil and thus I use it here as standing for moral evil. I realize that there might be some moral positions which do not associate moral evil with causing unnecessary pain, and for people who believe in these the argument of this paragraph will have little relevance.

attempt to imagine empathetically how he and others will feel as recipients of his act. How often does one hear "If only I had known, I never would have. . ." "If only I had foreseen . . . "I didn't realize you would feel this way about. . ."? If it is true that sensitive, thoughtful and imaginative people are less likely to cause unnecessary suffering than those who do not have these characteristics, then it is also true that the prudential person will tend not to be the immoral person. The real enemy of moral behavior is not the egoist who develops the required traits and abilities to find his own good; the real enemy is those persons who act only on their immediate feelings and impulses rather than on those motivations which come after thorough, sensitive and imaginative explorations of oneself and the situations in which one acts.

8.4  We are now in a position to answer that most important but elusive of questions:  "Why should a person be moral?" Let us assume that the only good reason for doing anything is that it is in one's best interests.[3] Although it is logically possible that one might always act in his best interests without ever knowing what those interests are, it is certainly dubious that this could happen in a world as precarious and complex as ours. In this world if one wishes to do that which is in his best interests, he needs to know what those interests are. However, as we have discovered, determining what one's interests are is a very difficult task and requires one to develop the skills of imagination, discerning facts, and reasoning logically and to cultivate the dispositions of objectivity, sensitivity, impartiality, and thoroughness. But if a person develops these abilities and traits fully, then they will make him take the moral point of view (see 8.2). Therefore, if one seeks what is in his best interests, then he must become a person who will think and act morally.

This argument does not maintain that in all cases taking the moral point of view is in one's best interests; it only says that it is in a person's interests to develop the kind of character which requires him to be moral. It may seem perverse to develop a character for prudential purposes which can then act against those purposes, but this is not so. Just because there

---

[3]If one does not wish to start with such an egoistic assumption, he need not, for the argument holds if one is seeking that which is in the interests of everyone or of a special group. The key to the argument is that in order to seek to fulfill the interests of any person or group one must know what those interests are and this will involve developing the moral abilities and dispositions.

are certain times when one's character might not act to further his interests does not mean that it is not in his interests to develop that character, for the only alternative to doing so involves far worse consequences. Not to develop this kind of character means that a person will not be able to determine what is in his best interests, and if one does not know what his interests are, then the chances that his acts will favor his interests will be entirely in the hands of fate, and there is no reason whatsoever to believe that fate will favor those interests. Thus, if a person finds himself not taking the moral point of view, this should indicate to him something which is very disturbing: that he is not the kind of person who knows what his own interests are or who can direct his life to its highest fulfillment.

8.5 One might now feel that something has gone awry, that our arguments have demonstrated too much, for while we started with the question of which point of view should take precedence when prudence and morals conflict, we have ended by negating prudence altogether as a possible stance. That is, we have discovered prudence to be an intrinsically self-destructive point of view--it always has to develop into the moral stance. But if morals is that point of view which deals basically with our actions that affect others, how are we to make decisions about our private existence? If prudence is impossible, then there seems to be no point of view from which to make those decisions which concern only our personal and private lives, and if this is so, then there must be something drastically wrong with the proposed theory.

This critique is valuable because it manifests a view that is both common and seriously mistaken. Can one divide his life into public and private spheres? Does not every act, every path taken have consequences both for oneself and for others? A person might think that he need consider only his own satisfaction in deciding what profession to enter, but this decision will certainly have profound effects on many other people. Even things done in the privacy of our own thoughts or chambers have effects for others, for they enter our habits, affect our personalities and moods, and provide us with more or less of what we can share with people. A person who holds that publicly he ought to try to make people happy while privately he is free to develop any kind of personality he wishes does not understand that who one is cannot be separated from how he affects other people. If the effects one has on others are in large part determined by the kind of character that he has and what one does in his solitariness affects the kind of character he develops, then a person cannot separate his private life from his public acts. How an agent decides to gain personal fulfillment, what he decides to do when he is alone, does affect other people and thus must be thought about morally.

If it is true that everything one does affects both himself and others, then we must find a mode of prescriptive thinking which combines both prudence and morals, which unites concern for one's own interests with concern for the interests of others. Such a mode of thinking is ethics. Ethics is not a point of view beyond morals; rather it is that level of moral thinking which (1) is grounded in an individual's understanding of his own interests, and which (2) requires that every practical decision one makes be the product of a moral exploration. Why call this kind of thinking 'ethics'? Why not just say that it is a high level of moral reasoning? For one, 'morals' has the traditional connotation of being a stance essentially concerned with one's relations to other people, and although the concept of morals presented in this book certainly does not imply that other people are more important recipients of one's acts than oneself is, it is very hard to free oneself of the notion that morals demands this view. On the other hand, 'ethics', in its sense of being that discipline which attempts to discover the principles of what it means to live a good life, is far more neutral as to whether others or oneself should be the central focus of prescriptive thought. Second, 'morals' frequently has the connotation (although not in this book) of being a point of view which needs to be invoked only in certain kinds of situations, such as in cases in which a moral rule might be broken or cases in which one's act has a direct effect on someone else's interests. There are times to be moral and times when one need not worry about it. 'Ethics,' however, has the sense of applying to everything one does because everything one does can be more or less part of a good life. For these reasons it will be semantically useful to designate as ethical thinking that level of moral reasoning which understands that oneself often is the most important recipient of one's acts and which sees that all the decisions and acts of one's life demand moral deliberation. The ethical person will be defined as someone who has developed the moral traits and abilities to a high degree and who has become a master of the art of ethical thinking.

The art of ethical thinking is based upon an agent's understanding and being sensitive to the interrelations of himself and his social and natural environments. It is a thinking which conceives the self not as an isolated entity, but as a being whose character and acts are always affecting its world and whose world is always affecting it. It is the kind of moral thinking which is centered on a knowledge of the agent's interests because in most cases it is the agent who is most keenly and drastically affected by his own decisions and acts, but which also realizes that a person cannot be separated from his environment and must become aware of its possibilities, limitations, and, most importantly, of the interests and feelings of the other people in it. Ethical thinking, then, is making one's

decisions about how to live and act only after one has completed
a factual and imaginative exploration of his own interests and
feelings, the interests and feelings of others, the various possible acts open to him, and how each of those acts will affect
both himself and others. To be able to gather these facts, empathetically imagine how oneself and others will feel as recipients
of one's possible acts, and then interweave all of these together
in the formation of a decision is, indeed, an art which we all
practice to some extent, but of which there are very few masters.

There is a metaphysic of human nature implied by this concept of ethical reasoning, and it is quite different from that
which underlies any ethic which bifurcates value decisions into
public and private spheres. The only concept of self which could
support a public-private ethic is a dualistic one in which the
self is divided into public and private parts. The most common
form of this type of theory is a mind-body dualism in which the
mind is totally private and subjective, while the body is that
through which public acts are made and received. Most of the
twentieth century philosophy in the West has strongly reacted
against such a dualism or any form of it in which either mind or
matter is seen as the ultimate reality. Rather than dualism,
twentieth century western philosophy is pervaded with the concept
of a person as a unified organism whose identity is intrinsically
connected with its social and natural environment. The concept
is most prevalent in American naturalism where James, Dewey,
Whitehead, and Mead have all emphasized that the interactions and
interrelations of the individual and his environment are the
fundamental reality of human existence, but it can also be found
in varying degrees in Wittgenstein's concept of man as a language-
using being, Strawson's notion of 'person,' and in the phenomeno-
logical tenet that man cannot be separated from his Lebenswelt.
It is this concept of a person as being constituted by his
interactions with his total environment that demands one develop
an art of ethical thinking in which he is required to interweave
reasoning and awareness of himself, others, and his world in
making decisions about how to live.

These concepts of the ethical person and ethical reasoning also have important implications for a philosophy of education.
If giving people an ability to determine what is good for themselves and what is good for the communities in which they live is
an important goal for education, then education must concern itself with nurturing the ethical virtues. For instance, rather
than just teaching facts, education should try to instill an
ability to discern facts--to abstract from a situation the properties which are relevant in making decisions about it. Rather
than having a format in which fairly dull and lifeless interactions occur between the members of a class, a mode of interaction should be developed in which sensitivity, impartiality,

and empathetic imagination can be learned and developed. Instead of emphasizing the memorization of data as the essential mode of thinking, exercises which call for the development of an ability to reason through difficult situations logically, imaginatively, and thoroughly ought to be given. These are, of course, mere suggestions, but they do indicate a way in which a great dilemma of moral education might be solved. The question is often raised as to whether educators ought to indoctrinate their students in what they consider to be right and wrong or whether they should allow their students to determine for themselves what values they ought to hold. The first method engenders dogmatism and passive receptivity; the second often is the cause of students being non-directed and engaging in destructive behavior. If instead of either of these paths, moral education attempted to cultivate in its students the abilities and traits needed in order for anyone to discover what is the best way to live, then this would neither be a dogmatic giving of values nor a totally chaotic "anything goes" policy. It would be that kind of education which the Greeks considered to be the most vital: the cultivation of a moral character.

8.6 Is this concept of the ethical person an ideal of what a person should be, an ideal of human excellence? If it is, it is at least not a moral or prudential ideal. That is, I am not saying that it is either prudentially or morally good to be a person with these definite traits and abilities. Such claims cannot be made because we do not know if such habits would always lead to the most satisfaction for every agent or would be valued as morally good by a being optimally taking the moral point of view. It seems that we can only hold the hypothetical imperative that if a person wants to be able to determine either what is in his own good or what is morally good, then he must develop the traits and abilities of the ethical person.

Yet, even though the concept of the ethical person cannot categorically be proven either morally or prudentially valid, there are conclusive reasons for saying that everyone ought to be an ethical person. If it is true that the only grounds upon which an action can be justified are either that it is in one's best interests or that it is the morally right thing to do, and if it is true that one cannot know what is in his best interests or what is morally right unless he develops the abilities and traits of an ethical person, then one ought to develop this kind of character. The only possible grounds for denying that one ought to develop the habits of the ethical person would be if one could show that such a character was morally or prudentially bad, and this cannot be done. It cannot be done because one can never be certain that he has found the correct prudential or moral principles and must, therefore, retain the character of the ethical person in order to be able to check and re-examine whether the principle he thinks is right can continuously meet the tests of the moral or prudential point of view. Thus, the 'ought' in the prescription "one ought to develop the traits and abilities of the ethical person" is neither a moral nor a prudential 'ought' but is rather the 'ought' of rational necessity: there are no possible grounds for saying that any other character ought to be developed.

But if this concept of the ethical person is being posited as an ideal which everyone should strive to attain, then does this not eliminate one of the crucial characteristics of ethical language: that a person must be free to make his own value choices: Again, this ideal is not being asserted as a moral or prudential value, but rather as the necessary ground for making any rational value judgment whatsoever. In this sense it is not limiting one's freedom to choose values but is providing a basis for such freedom to be meaningful and important. Also, this ideal of the ethical person is what I have called a formal ideal and not a material one. While it does state what kind of traits and abilities a person must have, it does not say what kind of life he should lead or what kinds of experiences he should seek. It gives a basis from which such experiences can be chosen but does not dictate what those choices must be. An ethical person could hold another ideal, such as seeking a height of aesthetic intensity or being as altruistic as possible. He might be a businessman, a poet, housewife, bum, mechanic, king or pauper. But the one thing he cannot do is choose a kind of life or set of experiences that would negate his ethical virtues. Freedom to choose one's values is essential if a person is to be an autonomous being controlling the direction and course of his life, but this freedom is meaningful only if it is exercised by someone capable of making informed, concerned, and intelligent decisions. We are free to choose our values, but never free to choose against the ideal of living in the most sensitive, imaginative, impartial, and rational way possible for us to attain.

# INDEX

## ABOUT THE AUTHOR

John Riker, now in his mid-thirties, has been a professor of philosophy at Colorado College for the last ten years. He did his undergraduate work at Middlebury College and received his advanced degrees in philosophy at Vanderbilt University. His concerns in philosophy are broad with strong interests in analytic philosophy, existentialism, American naturalism and pragmatism, Whitehead, and the Classical Greeks. Along with being a dedicated teacher and scholar, Professor Riker also takes an active role in the community life of Colorado College and Colorado Springs where he has been president of the local ACLU chapter and chairman of the Colorado Springs Choral Society Board. In the summer he can usually be found backpacking in the mountains of Colorado with his wife and two sons. The Art of Ethical Thinking is his first book.

JOHN RIKER

Photo by
Peter Bahnsen